STRENGTHS-BASED COUNSELING
WITH AT-RISK YOUTH

STRENGTHS-BASED COUNSELING

WITH AT-RISK YOUTH

MICHAEL UNGAR

CORWIN PRESS
A SAGE Publications Company
Thousand Oaks, California

For information:

Corwin Press
A Sage Publications Company
2455 Teller Road
Thousand Oaks, California 91320
www.corwinpress.com

Sage Publications Ltd.
1 Oliver's Yard
55 City Road
London EC1Y 1SP
United Kingdom

Sage Publications India Pvt. Ltd.
B-42, Panchsheel Enclave
Post Box 4109
New Delhi 110 017 India

Printed in the United States of America.

Library of Congress Cataloging-in-Publication Data

Ungar, Michael, 1963-
Strengths-based counseling with at-risk youth / Michael Ungar.
       p. cm.
Includes bibliographical references and index.
ISBN 1-4129-2819-2 (cloth) — ISBN 1-4129-2820-6 (pbk.)
    1. Youth with social disabilities—Services for. 2. Problem youth—Services for. I. Title.
HV1421.U54 2006
616.89′00835—dc22

                                                                2005025358

This book is printed on acid-free paper.

06   07   08   09   10   9   8   7   6   5   4   3   2   1

Acquisitions Editor:	Stacy Wagner
Production Editor:	Jenn Reese
Copy Editor:	Marilyn Power Scott
Typesetter:	C&M Digitals (P) Ltd.
Proofreader:	Caryne Brown
Cover Designer:	Rose Storey
Graphic Designer:	Lisa Miller

Contents

Preface   vii

Acknowledgments   xi

About the Author   xiii

1. **Surviving and Thriving**   1
   The Many Ways Youth Survive   2
   Three Survival Strategies, Three Identities   4
   Power and Self-Definition   6
   Substitution as Intervention   7
   Narrative Interventions   11
   Powerful Alternatives   13

2. **Three Identities: Pandas, Chameleons, and Leopards**   17
   The Stuck Panda   18
   The Uncertain Chameleon   25
   The Demanding Leopard   28
   Pegs and Holes   32

3. **Six Strategies for Nurturing Resilience**   35
   Overview of the Six Strategies   36
   Paths to Resilience: Conventional
   and Unconventional   37
   Strategy 1: Hear Their Truth   40

4. **From Truth to Action: Implementing
   Strategies Two Through Five**   49
   Strategy 2: Help Youth Look Critically
   at Their Behavior   50
   Strategy 3: Create Opportunities That Fit With
   What Youth Say They Need   54

Strategy 4: Speak in Ways Youth Will
   Hear and Respect   57
Strategy 5: Find the Difference
   That Counts the Most   61

5. The Many Expressions of Youth Resilience   **69**
   Strategy 6: Substitute Rather Than Suppress   70
   Substitutions for Drug Use   72
   Substitutions for Other At-Risk Behaviors   75
   The Many Expressions of Resilience   76

6. A New Way to Look at Bullying   **81**
   Bullying as Coping: Jake   82
   Bullying and the Three Identities   90
   Providing Opportunities for Adaptation   92
   Substitutions for Bullies   93
   Substitutions for Victims   94

7. Assessing Resilience   **97**
   The Resilient Youth Strengths Inventory   98
   Evaluating Fairly   107

8. Translating the Results of the Resilient
   Youth Strengths Inventory   **111**
   Pandas Shoot   112
   Chameleons Score   113
   Leopards Win   113
   Using Results to Inform Our Efforts   118

Conclusion: The Need for Change   **121**

References   **123**

Index   **126**

Preface

There on the front page of *The Daily News* in Halifax, Nova Scotia, was the headline that I knew was coming: "'Loser' kills one at Alberta School" (1999), announcing another shooting at a high school just days after the mass shooting at Columbine in Boulder, Colorado. I had said to friends and family after I heard about Columbine that it would be only a matter of time and there would be another copycat incident.

Sadly, I was wrong. There hasn't been *just* one, but many similar incidents. There have also been literally thousands of threats heard throughout schools and other public institutions from youth who feel as if they have nothing to lose and everything to gain by acting violently. It was that bolded word "Loser" in the headline that made it all so inevitable.

Thanks to the miracle of mass media, that young boy thousands of miles from Columbine was shown exactly what he could do if he wanted instant notoriety. *We* handed him the script. In a world where there are few options for such a dramatic shift in identity, this loser found a way out of a lifetime of stigma and exclusion. If he had instead found a group of similarly disenfranchised youth who had managed other ways to make the same statement, could he have borrowed from them some of their status to shore up his own flagging self-image? Was there no other alternative to violence and murder?

Of course we could blame his family or his teachers for allowing him to be bullied. Or if we are of a different political stripe, we could argue that he would have been deterred from his crime if only we had harsher punishments for young offenders. We might debate issues of gun control and speculate on how we ever let a boy his age in his state of mind get hold of a gun. But the sad truth is that none of these political and ideological musings will solve the problems kids face. The truth is that while that boy may have been a loser before, he will from this point on have a much more powerful identity, one partly of his own design but one that shares the status given a growing number of school-aged children: "Murderer."

This book is about preventing these tragedies, both great and small. Young people don't have to cope with their problems by becoming violent or acting out in other socially unacceptable ways. Over the years, adolescents and their families have shown me that they survive best when they are helped to find healthy and *powerful* identities that others recognize both at school and at home. This approach to "problem" youth, whether they are acting out violently or simply beginning to cause their teachers and caregivers worry, offers hope. It looks beyond the psychopathology and bad behavior of our youth to better understand them and their ways of coping as adaptive, no matter how irrational their behavior may seem at the time. This book is meant as a roadmap through the facade of dangerous, delinquent, deviant, and disordered behaviors found among troubled kids. It will show that educators, like parents and other adults, still play a large part in the lives of these teenagers and, what's more, that teenagers want and need adults to be there for them.

How to Use This Book

This book will help you to look at youth differently. It begins with a discussion of problem youth, offering an innovative way of seeing them as *pandas, chameleons* and *leopards.* These three "labels" are ways youth and I have found to describe young people's patterns of coping and surviving. Pandas are stuck with one pattern, chameleons adapt to the environments they find themselves in, while leopards change the environments around them. The first two chapters will share many stories about these youth, including my own experience as a teenager, in order to show how kids use these coping strategies to nurture and maintain resilience. Chapters 3 through 5 provide six strategies that I use in my work with troubled youth and their teachers and families. Each strategy builds on the strengths youth show as pandas, chameleons, and leopards, encouraging a more positive and individualized understanding of why youth act out in troubling ways. There is much in these chapters for educators and caregivers struggling to find the tools necessary to help the youth in their care.

Chapter 6 applies these strategies to kids who bully. There are a number of problems that could be discussed. Bullying, however, like other forms of violence, is one of those pervasive problems that we are struggling to address in our schools and communities. Looking at bullies as pandas, chameleons, and leopards and applying the six strategies for intervention will bring together all the ideas presented in earlier chapters into a comprehensive model of strengths-based intervention.

Chapters 7 and 8 provide a short assessment tool, the Resilient Youth Strengths Inventory, for educators and caregivers of problem kids. The tool is not meant to add the label of resilient or nonresilient to individual youth; it is instead a checklist of items we should examine when we consider how best to help our children become more resilient. In the discussion that follows the presentation of the Inventory, I stress the need to see even problem behavior as signs of resilience in contexts that lack resources for healthy development. Scoring the Inventory helps us to appreciate the unique solutions our young people use to survive.

A Collaborative Effort With Young People

None of the ideas in this book are mine alone. The adolescents and families whom I have met along the way have been my greatest teachers. It had to be that way. How else could I have come to understand something as complex as the way teens find healthy and powerful identities without listening closely to their own stories?

It is too easy to make assumptions as adults that the way we perceive the world is how the world is. It is changing as we breathe. The many youth who shared their lives with me and my colleagues who helped to clarify my thinking all played an important part in crystallizing a snapshot of how youth survive *and thrive* despite the adversity they face.

This book is about resilience as it is negotiated between people. It is not just a checklist for what to do and not do to help kids. It is not meant to pigeonhole kids into categories so that we can feel comfortable with the labels we assign them, though I do use labels that kids themselves have helped me create. My hope is that by using the six strategies I discuss, others will come to hear the same stories of strength I have been privileged to have had shared with me.

Note: The Youth and Their Families

In order to protect the privacy of all the individuals with whom I have had the privilege to work, the reader must know that the stories I share in these pages are both real and imagined, based on bits and pieces of lives lived, cobbled together from anecdotes common to the many young people and their families that I have met through my research and clinical practice. Each of the composite sketches of youth and their families that appear are substitutes for individuals whose identities must, of course, remain confidential. None of the people portrayed actually exist as I describe them, though some readers might think they recognize in these pages someone in particular. I would suggest the resemblance is more coincidence than fact.

Perhaps, if the stories sound familiar, it is because throughout my career in a number of communities, big and small, I have met hundreds of youth who shared much in common with one another. My hope is that readers find here stories that ring true for them and those for whom they care.

Acknowledgments

Corwin Press gratefully acknowledges the contributions of the following people:

Bonnie Benard, Senior Program Associate, WestEd, Oakland, CA

Dana L. Edwards, Assistant Professor, Department of Counseling and Psychological Services, Georgia State University

William P. Evans, Professor and State Specialist for Youth Development, Human Development and Family Studies, University of Nevada, Reno

Edward L. James, Educational Consultant, Appling, GA

John Winslade, Associate Professor and Program Coordinator for Educational Counseling, Department of Educational Psychology and Counseling, California State University, San Bernardino

About the Author

Michael Ungar, PhD, is both a social worker and marriage and family therapist with experience working directly with children, youth, and adults in mental health, educational, and correctional settings. Now an associate professor at the School of Social Work, at Dalhousie University in Halifax, Canada, he continues to supervise and consult extensively with educators, guidance counselors, and other professionals across North America and overseas in countries such as Russia, China, Tanzania, and Colombia. Dr. Ungar has appeared on numerous national and regional radio and television shows and is a frequent lecturer and keynote speaker at conferences for child psychiatrists, social workers, psychologists, school guidance counselors, family therapists, and other mental health professionals, as well as parents and foster parents.

He has conducted many workshops internationally on resilience-related themes relevant to the treatment and study of at-risk youth and has published dozens of peer-reviewed articles on resilience and work with children and their families. He is also the author of three books. His first, *Playing at Being Bad*, is a book for parents. A second publication, for therapists, is titled *Nurturing Hidden Resilience in Troubled Youth*. His third, the *Handbook for Working With Children and Youth: Pathways to Resilience Across Cultures and Contexts*, is an edited volume with 56 international contributors.

Ungar holds numerous research grants from national funding bodies and is a collaborator on several international research projects as well. He is Lead Investigator of the 11-country, 5-continent International Resilience Project (www.resilienceproject.org), an international collaboration that includes researchers, community practitioners, and children's rights advocates internationally.

1

Surviving and Thriving

It is not the person who is the problem. Rather, it is the problem that is the problem.

—Michael White

Geoffrey looked like a cuddly bear: A big mop of reddish hair that never seemed to be combed, freckles, a little fleshy around the arms and midriff in the way adolescent boys get when their appetites are healthy, their bodies about to sprout, and their diet chosen from a seemingly endless snack bar of potato chips, soft drinks, and pizza. When I was in junior high he sat at the back of my Grade 7 home-room. He'd sit slouched, his legs spread, doodling. Most days, he seemed completely inoffensive, just another mediocre student whom teachers might have forgotten if not for his knack of finding victims for his cruelty.

I often think about Geoffrey and how he treated me. In a way, we remained glued to one another for the first three months of Grade 7. Geoffrey needed someone's shoulders to stand on. He needed someone that he could put down, intimidate, and tease. He needed this someone if he was going to find some way out of that cesspool of mediocrity that breeds hopelessness and invisibility among lower-class kids from stable, rural communities who don't excel at school.

Geoffrey knew he was going nowhere. His solution, it seemed, was to defiantly make a claim to whatever fame he could find close at hand.

I was an easy mark. I had been advanced a grade when I moved from Montréal to a small northern community just before I turned 11. I was a little smaller than the other boys the year Geoffrey and I met in that first year of junior high. I did well at school. I liked to focus on projects as they came along. I was a volunteer reporter for a local newspaper. Most days, teachers liked me or, at the very least, they could ignore me in favor of students who needed more attention.

The Many Ways Youth Survive

Similar Backgrounds, Different Behaviors

The strange thing was that the families Geoffrey and I came from weren't that different. Geoffrey lived in a working-class home with a stay-at-home mom. There were rumors that his older brothers got in trouble with the police and that his father was an alcoholic.

I was from a working-class family that was creeping into the middle class. My father, a quiet man, had supported himself and my mother sweeping factory floors while he finished high school studying at night. We had our own secrets, though, ones far less public than drinking. For years, my mother coped with depression, a socially isolated, mildly abusive woman who experienced life secondhand through television and a make-believe world of friends. Before my father retired, he found it best to be absent a great deal of the time, maintaining respectability by spending his time at work, a content workaholic.

But of course, Geoffrey didn't know any of this about me. We were new to the community, and a year after arriving, I still remained relatively unknown to my peers, who were now mostly older than me. Geoffrey's abusive behavior toward me made the first three months of seventh grade a long, horrendous slog. Stomach aches didn't get me out of going to class. Hiding during lunch didn't avoid the taunts, punches, and threats as I was routinely routed out of my quiet spaces and forced to be on the playground by well-intentioned, rule-abiding teachers. I said nothing of course about what I was experiencing.

Doing Whatever It Takes

I'd like to say that this was all one awful experience, but I can't. Instead, I owe Geoffrey some measure of thanks. He planted the seed of an idea that would take another 25 years to bloom. Looking back now at Geoffrey, I see *he wasn't a bad kid acting bad* but a kid like me who each morning rose out of bed and made the simple promise to himself: "Today I'm going to do whatever I have to do to survive!" And he did. He survived quite well, given the resources he had.

> In our haste to change our children's behavior, we overlook how those behaviors make sense to children themselves. Try as we might as adults to guide children, they will not heed our words of advice until they are confident we understand they are already doing the best they can with what they have.

Resilience

Geoffrey taught me what *resilience* really is. I'm not sure I would have used that word when I was in seventh grade, but I have certainly learned since that people survive in many different ways, eking out their best existence from the resources they have at hand. Typically, we speak about resilience as people's capacity to overcome great adversity in their lives. Resilient children tend to fall into two groups: those who beat the odds and those who *more than* beat the odds.

Beating the Odds

> Resilient kids *beat the odds* when they achieve success equal to kids who face far fewer problems (Fraser, 1997). These students are the ones who grow up confronting many and varied challenges: some that are *acute,* occurring just once, like sexual abuse or the death of a parent; others that are *chronic* and part of their daily lives. These might include physical abuse, dangerous home neighborhoods, underfunded schools, poverty, or an ill caregiver.

More Than Beating the Odds

> The resilient students who *more than beat the odds* manage to rise above their adversity, learn from it, and thrive beyond all expectations. Sometimes we call them *invulnerables* (Anthony, 1987). Though that term is a misnomer, as these adolescents too struggle to cope, they garner our admiration nonetheless.

Children grow and children change. They will move in and out of roles as easily as they slip on and off ponies on the merry-go-round. Surviving will mean one thing one day, something novel and new the next. The only certainty is uncertainty.

Through all these changes, adolescents tell me, through my clinical work and research, that they seek something special to say about themselves, something that will bring with its next revolution the hopes of *power* and *acceptance* (Ungar & Teram, 2000).

Three Survival Strategies, Three Identities

When we understand what young people tell us, we can see the reasonableness in how they choose to behave. Some remain stuck in patterns, making the most of the one or two things they do well. I call these adolescents, with their permission, *pandas*. After all, panda bears have very little capacity to change. No matter where they find themselves, they will eat only a few varieties of bamboo or perish. They simply cannot adapt, which is why encroachment on their traditional mountain territory in China has proved so fatal to their numbers.

A second group of adolescents are more adaptable but less secure. They change with each new situation they enter, experimenting with new identities but unable to assert who they are exactly. These teenagers are like *chameleons*, those lizardlike creatures that are uncannily adept at changing their skin color to fit in any environment, matching even elaborate and colorfully patterned backgrounds.

Finally, a third group of adolescents appear to have a sure-footed sense of themselves. These are the *leopards*, young people who seem to confidently assert who they are and demand of the world that it regards them in a particular way. I look at these teenagers and think of the languid leopard at rest on the lower branches of a tree, its relaxed stature hiding a more powerful, dangerous capacity to survive and adapt. There are many different breeds of leopards, but each is capable of making its way in several different climates.

THREE SURVIVAL STRATEGIES

Children use three strategies to create powerful identities:

> ➤ Pandas stick with one identity no matter where they are or whom they are with.
> ➤ Chameleons blend in to survive.
> ➤ Leopards insist others look at them in ways they control.

Young people who act like one or the other of these animals may behave in ways we like or dislike, depending on how much we accept the adolescent's behavior as reasonable and, given the circumstances (such as whether the behavior occurs in a classroom or on the playground), acceptable. Regardless of what the youth are doing, these three approaches to life help the young people cope with the challenges of nurturing and maintaining a powerful way of being themselves when they're with others.

> We may judge the panda bear for not changing its diet, but we don't condemn the panda for doing what it does best. Nor do we judge the chameleon for being inconsistent or the leopard for its forthrightness. Our teens are less fortunate. We insist they conform, do as we tell them, behave as we adults see fit. This us-them thinking, of course, gets us nowhere.

Embracing Change

Adolescents, whether they act like pandas and are stuck with one identity, resemble chameleons constantly changing how they are known to others, or have the assertiveness and adaptability of leopards, are all quite normal. Each role may be expressed in ways we like or dislike. After all, adults are pandas, chameleons, and leopards, too. Just look at what we drive, where we live, and who we have as friends. For some, the chameleons and leopards, there is a great deal of variation in the faces they present to the world and how they want to be known. These are the people new-car sellers love, always trading in mildly used vehicles for the latest in automobile looks.

Let's face it: The "problem" kids we meet in our classrooms and offices often remind us that we were once wild and foolish, too. We experimented with different ways of expressing ourselves. I sometimes wonder if we are most upset with adolescents because they challenge us adults to let down our guard, to be a little less certain of how the world ought to be. Kahlil Gibran (1923/1982), who wrote the pithy wisdom of *The Prophet,* tells us, "What of the old serpent who cannot shed his skin, and calls all others naked and shameless?" (p. 36). Our children perplex us with their stick-to-itiveness. They also perplex us when they rapidly change. "Why can't they just do as I say?" we wonder. What happened, though, to our own transitory ways of trying on new identities?

> Adults look at change as something to be feared. Kids look at change as something they can't avoid. To cope with the inevitable, our children need practice playing different roles behind different masks. Our job as their educators and caregivers is to provide the opportunities for them to experiment with new identities.

Power and Self-Definition

In Their Own Words

Without the blinders placed in front of us by our biases as adults, it can be interesting to look closely at what young people and their peer groups can teach us about health, identity, and the stories we create for ourselves that direct our lives. If we are to debunk an old myth about all youth who rebel being problem kids, then we will need a more powerful story that tells us how things really are. The more we encounter teenagers' identities as they want them to be known, those they build both inside and outside our classrooms, the more successful we will likely be hearing their powerful truths.

The young people whose stories are recounted in this book help us reconsider what we believe about young people and why. The wisdom of our youth can provide the foundation for a new myth about adolescents and their drift toward health. Like March storms that signal the impending shift in climate from one season to the next, problem behaviors among both children and teenagers can just as often be harbingers of resilience, when we take the time to hear their stories told in their own words.

Choosing Labels

When we hand over some control of the definition of mental health to teens, we learn that they and their peer groups do whatever they need to do to stay healthy and accepted and to experience themselves as powerful in their relationships with others. This power is not a power *over* others but a mutual and diffuse power that philosophers like Michel Foucault (1972/1980) have called "capillary." In much the same way as the small capillaries in our lungs each play an important part in drawing oxygen into our bloodstreams, so too do we each as individuals play a part in deciding who is powerful and who is not.

In practical terms this means that as we perform our roles in society, we add our voices to how our community describes us and others. If I am a bully, like Geoffrey, then I am likely to experience different understandings of that word, adding my voice to the majority (or minority) of others in deciding whether being a bully is something good or bad. Among Geoffrey's closest friends, being a bully meant being powerful. This idea of the bully as powerful, of course, is not shared by everyone. And Geoffrey knew it. To most people, to be called a bully is an insult. Still, it is likely that to Geoffrey's mind, being a bully was a darned sight better label to carry than the alternatives accessible to him, which, I suspect, may have appeared to him to be invested with even less power. Who, after all, wants to be known as a "dumb kid"?

The good news is that most youth want powerful self-definitions but not at the expense of others losing theirs. The problem is that in a world where we hold to the myth that power is scarce, we have come to believe that our happiness must come at the expense of another's. In fact, in a recent study of university students, participants in small groups were asked if they would rather receive $50,000 and everyone else in their group $25,000 or receive $100,000 and everyone else $200,000. The majority of students chose the first option (Dr. Richard Laynard, cited in Anderssen, 2004). Their happiness was directly related to the lower status of others.

And yet, the troubled teens whom I routinely interview tell me they are far more accepting of others' self-definitions as powerful *when that respect is reciprocated*. At least among the troubled teens I meet, their attitude seems to be "take the money and run," caring little about their status when compared with others their own age. As long as they have something unique and powerful to say about themselves as individuals, they are content. This, like much of what these teens have taught me, goes against our conventional wisdom about problem teens and what they are thinking.

Substitution as Intervention

It is for this reason that I promote tolerance of teenagers' at times problematic decisions about how they are going to achieve resilience. Teens have shown me that behaviors I oppose are seldom corrected more than momentarily through coercion. Instead, I prefer to understand their behavior as a *search for health*. My belief is that we must *substitute rather than suppress*.

I seek ways to offer youth alternatives to dangerous, delinquent, deviant, and disordered behavior. Alternatives must, however, offer the same quality of experience that the young person achieved through his or her problem behavior.

As I will show, bullying and other problem behaviors as diverse as drug use, sexual promiscuity, and truancy are all attractive to adolescents because they satisfy the youth's need for power, recreation, acceptance, or a sense of meaningful participation in his or her community, to name just a few of the benefits that adolescents tell me (and research supports) come from problem behaviors. If I am to help young people move away from these behaviors, I must understand the good things that teens say they derive from being bad. When I fall short of understanding the good reasons for problem behaviors among students inside and outside the classroom, I fall short of offering alternatives that draw youth to take advantage of new opportunities.

Teenagers more often *run toward* something powerful and sustaining than *away from* that which threatens their well-being.

SUBSTITUTION

By helping teens substitute one identity for another, we fulfill three purposes:

➢ We draw them into new, positive behaviors by offering them practical ways to experience themselves in different but powerful identities.
➢ We create an opportunity for those who know (and often fear or dislike) the students to appreciate them through new identities that demonstrate their attributes.
➢ We become the ally rather than the enemy, as they are drawn toward those who can offer powerful and socially acceptable identity substitutes.

Trading Up

If we are going to stop our students' chaotic behavior in our classrooms, on our playgrounds, and in our communities, we are going to have to trade them conventional but *powerful* opportunities to show themselves as healthy and in control of their lives for their unconventional and destructive sources of strength. What we offer must provide them with much the same benefits they derive from unconventional strategies for health. Finding that which is equal but more socially acceptable is often difficult because it must be tailor-made to meet each young person's needs. Fortunately, good educators often know exactly what a student needs. The problem is more often the structural constraints that prevent schools and their administrators from being either able or willing to adapt on a case-by-case basis.

Christine

Fourteen-year-old Christine lives in a group home most days. It's not her choice, but she tolerates her placement because she knows life at home would be worse: no food, a mother struggling with alcoholism, an abusive father who is rumored to have been involved in a rash of recent corner store thefts. Christine survives by trying to fit in. She is a reluctant chameleon, more comfortable playing the hard-to-reach teen, with lots of attitude and a dismissive way of treating her teachers. But she knows she needs help, too. She doesn't want to repeat the mistakes of her mother. The trouble is, she doesn't really know how else to make her life work.

When we met, it was through a referral from her guidance counselor. Christine needed more help than could be managed by someone with a caseload of 1,500 kids. It was a shame, as her counselor would likely have been better placed to help Christine find a new and powerful identity. In the end we worked together, with the counselor attending sessions whenever she could.

> Most days after school, Christine drifts out on to the streets in her old neighborhood, 10 blocks from her group home, which is on the edge of a middle-class suburb. Christine prefers her old school, her old friends, and her old lifestyle, even though it places her at greater risk. She has already contracted one sexually transmitted disease and thought she was pregnant. She's had black eyes from brawls with other girls. She smokes. The police who walk the beat in her old neighborhood know her by name, a point of pride for Christine.

Christine told me that she's comfortable on those streets, and life is predictable. The biggest challenge, she says, is finding a place to be as the evenings turn cold and dark.

School is an interruption in her day. She explained that she goes because she has to, or else she can't stay at her group home. The alternative is an even more restrictive housing arrangement, a mental health treatment center. She refers to it as the "kiddie jail."

What surprised me, though, was that Christine went to school at all. Though she was frequently given detentions, rarely (if ever) completed her homework, and rarely went a week without skipping one class or another, she still attended. She says she liked her homeroom social studies teacher. When I asked her why, despite all the other problems she has in her life, she sticks with school, she grunted, "I dunno." But later, she warmed a bit.

"What happens at school that is different from the rest of your life?" I tried again. This time she answered.

"Mr. Makhnach notices when I'm not there. It's like he sees me. No one else does, really. Even at the group home, it's all rules."

The topic Mr. Makhnach taught helped, too. Social studies interested Christine, who liked standing on her soapbox and arguing with everyone about how things really were "out there." She wasn't shy about her life, even if she didn't know quite what to do to change it.

"Sometimes I'll have to straighten my teacher out on things. He's not from here. Maybe the Ukraine or around there. So he doesn't know much about kids. And the other kids in the class are always making fun of him, but at least he's not all friggin' high on himself. I don't hassle him. But we're all pretty much on his case if he thinks all we do is smoke pot or if he imagines no one is sexually active, stuff like that. Then we have to like say, 'Look, it's like this, you know.' And he listens."

More important, he listens as Christine tries on her new identity as social activist, educating her educators about the realities of today's youth. Mr. Makhnach gives her space to speak, to play the expert rather than the problem kid.

Christine's guidance counselor met with us after a few sessions. We talked more about Christine's time with Mr. Makhnach. No one had known how much she liked him. It helped to change Christine's educational plan. Whereas the school had been threatening to suspend her permanently and move her to a special school for disruptive youth, this glimmer of hope encouraged them to extend themselves further to include Christine more in the life of the school. As remarkable as it sounds, she was invited to participate in a tutoring program for young children from her neighborhood. As long as it meant time away from her seventh grade studies, she was happy to participate and showed a natural talent for engaging with younger children. "I have two younger brothers, after all," she said when I asked her what made her so good at tutoring.

The Remarkably Unremarkable

Even more important, we spoke with Mr. Makhnach—*with Christine's permission.* A quiet man, he was astounded to hear that Christine was so taken with his class. He felt he did nothing out of the ordinary to engage with her. He only knew her as a slightly "brazen, outspoken" girl whose attendance was sporadic. He liked her and knew she liked the subject he taught, but beyond that, she had not made as significant an impression on him as he had on her.

Odd, we all thought, the way adolescents migrate to what they need, finding what they must in the most unlikely places. We invited Christine's teacher to speak with Christine about her participation in the class. He invited her to help with a community food bank project he was trying to start. Remarkably, Christine accepted the invitation.

> Youth will accept our invitations to change when what we offer is as satisfying to them as their less conventional pursuits.

My work with Christine ended a few sessions later. She wasn't looking for counseling about her family. She was looking for a place to belong, first. I left the door open, instead, and encouraged her to talk with her guidance counselor or teacher if she ever needed to get out of a tough situation. I suggested that since they saw her as a competent young woman, they would be honored to be asked for help from someone who knew so much about surviving. I also invited her counselor and teacher to ask Christine for help whenever they needed advice about how things "really were" in the community beyond the school's fence.

Narrative Interventions

This work with Christine is typical of the kinds of conversations I have with adolescents and the teachers and counselors who work with them. In the pages that follow, I will discuss a number of strategies that worked well with Christine and how one can put these into practice in one's own work with "problem" students.

This approach builds on what has come to be known as postmodern approaches to counseling, theorized by psychologists like Kenneth Gergen (2001) and Sheila McNamee (McNamee & Gergen, 1992) and social workers like Adrienne Chambon (Chambon & Irving, 1994), among many others. More recently, their ideas have been developed into clinical, educational, and community approaches to helping by Michael White (2000), John Winslade and Gerald Monk (1999), Alice Morgan (2000), David Epston (White & Epston, 1990), David Nylund (Nylund & Ceske, 1997; Nylund & Corsiglia, 1996), and a host of others who sometimes call themselves "narrative therapists." Collectively, we are finding better ways to engage with youth that avoid the resistance typically encountered by well-intentioned but unsuccessful professional helpers, whether teachers, counselors, social workers, psychologists, or child and youth care workers with a mandate to intervene.

The Four D's of "Problem" Teens

Teenagers who get the most attention in our communities are those who are either dangerous, delinquent, deviant, or disordered. Often they carry more than one of these labels. Interventionists using narrative techniques see each of these problems as a story, told over time, and supported by those with the power to label these youth as "problem teens." Each label velcros to the young person, on the one hand limiting the youth's options and on the other providing a perfect script for how to act out his or her vulnerability. Youth the world over who are convinced that they are dangerous, delinquent, deviant, or disordered will play each role for all its worth. And why not? When options are few, adolescents tell me, they make do with what they have.

Dangerous Youth

These are young people who scare us with the risks they take, potentially harming themselves or others. They drive motorbikes too quickly, pull pranks, experiment with fire setting, engage in unprotected sex, run away, and show all kinds of other reckless behavior that endangers themselves and their peers. Dangerous youth are those who have usually avoided jail or the stigma of a mental health diagnosis.

Delinquent Youth

Youth identified with the justice system or likely to be involved with police and the courts are called delinquents. The delinquent youth has broken a law or is dangerously close to breaking the law. These are the youth who shoplift—or worse, steal cars. They get into brawls and bully. They may even drift into prostitution or selling drugs as ways to survive on the street.

Deviant Youth

These youth are social misfits. They are the ones that break with social norms. They may have also broken the law and may have a mental health problem. More often, though, they simply do things the rest of their community feels uncomfortable about. Unfortunately, in some communities, being outwardly gay, lesbian, or bisexual is enough to earn the label. In other communities, it is street youth who are called deviants, or children who hide in their rooms endlessly surfing the Net. We mustn't forget, though, that what we label deviance changes over time and across cultures.

Disordered Youth

Youth who are categorized as disordered either have a diagnosis as mentally ill or are likely to be diagnosed with a mental health problem. Disorders are frequently used to explain the adolescent's deviance, delinquency, or dangerousness. Conduct disorder and Attention Deficit Hyperactivity Disorder are ubiquitous labels found among problem kids. More seriously, there are also children who appear to be "borderline" or "narcissistic" and who have problems "attaching." The label of disordered, however, is never entirely scientific, as what is or is not a sign of mental illness constantly changes.

Often these youths' schools, communities, families, and the professionals in their lives hand them ready-made life stories based on the labels they carry. These stories youth tell about themselves are coauthored and elaborately negotiated between the adolescent and those who are special in their lives.

Powerful Alternatives

As a first principle for helping youth find healthier identities, ones we associate with resilience, whether as pandas, chameleons, or leopards, adolescents must find substitutes for their problem behaviors. Whether we like to admit it or not, for Christine, truancy and everything else gave her a sense of control over her life. It provided her with a status among her peers that she would never achieve academically or through sports. She liked the way her friends looked at her. She liked the way she could survive.

Finding a substitute meant placing in front of her something of equal value. Once her mouthy, defiant personality found a niche, a place where it could perform in a conventional way, she was drawn there like a moth to a flame. Problem behaviors will extinguish much more easily when there is a substitute.

Alternatives Must Be Chosen, Not Required

Despite beliefs by some adults, there is no evidence that interventions that try to force kids to stop behaviors work. They stop smoking not because they are told to stop but when there are alternatives that bring the same experience, are a better use of their money, and are supported by their audience, both peers and adults, who see them as being just as cool, just as adult, and just as much in control of their own lives as when they smoke. Is it any wonder then that cell phones have caught on so well even as cigarette use is declining? Both trade in the same currency: an adultlike social activity that breeds an image as hip.

The same goes with sex. Abstinence will be a draw only for those kids attracted to the alternative: identification with a lifestyle or set of religious beliefs that replaces the cachet that sexual activity brings. We are mistaken if we think admonishing behavior stops kids. It is offering them a well-considered alternative that is key to successful interventions.

Figure 1.1 plots the relationship between socially acceptable and "problem" identity choices. Pandas, chameleons, and leopards are precariously balanced between these choices, pulled in one direction or the other by how others see them and how they see themselves. To the extent that we as educators and caregivers intervene with a prosocial substitute for problem behaviors, the more likely we are to tip the balance and provide the opportunities for youth to gently move their way toward identities as teenagers who survive and thrive (are resilient) in ways that don't harm themselves or others.

Figure 1.1   Identity Choices for Pandas, Chameleons, and Leopards

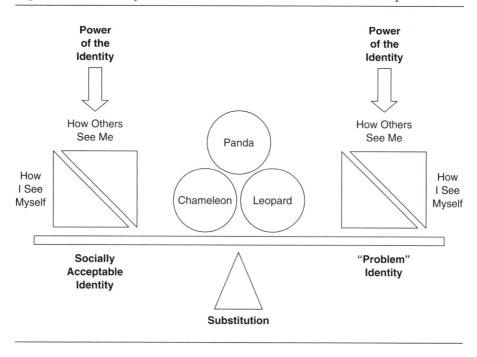

Negative Alternatives Make for Fierce Competition

It's not always quite so easy to find alternatives. What can we *really* offer a student who is dealing drugs on the playground and who tells everyone to f___ off at the slightest provocation? Frankly, if we admit the truth, most times we have little else to offer than mediocre prospects to achieve minimal grades, a high school diploma, and a service-industry or manual-labor job that pays minimum wage.

> If we are honest, sometimes we have little to offer young people that will bring them as much power, as much status, and as much wealth as they find through their problem behaviors. Admitting this to them is the first step to helping youth look for alternatives that are realistically available.

Jamie

Jamie is only 12, but already he has adult-sized problems. He has been running drugs for years for some older boys in his neighborhood. Once he himself came of age and he could be charged with possession, he decided it was better to jump in fully and begin selling for himself. After all, he had ready access to children his own age. He was, at least at first, rather invisible when buying and selling leftover Ritalin, pot, and anything else that he could find a market for.

Jamie's father worries about him and is willing to come in anytime school personnel phone. However, there isn't much that the adults can agree to offer Jamie except stricter rules and school expulsions. The first he laughs at; the second he encourages, as it gives him more time to hang out and develop his criminal capital, learning from older kids how to make something of himself as a delinquent.

The school, to its credit, has tried to do what it can. It's offered Jamie the opportunity to play sports and fund his equipment. Staff have invited him into programs for peer mediators. They've made extra tutors available and made sure no one teased him when he was forced to meet with a remedial reading specialist.

None of the multifaceted efforts worked, because none of those options were able to draw Jamie away from his street life. When I met him in jail after he'd been caught for possession, he told me, "What do I care? I had all that weed in my pocket. I had my own money. I was so far out in front of the other kids. They got nothing that I want. But I have what they want."

Jamie wasn't about to give it all up. He'd watched his father struggle to make ends meet. His mother had left him with his dad when he was three. His stepmother was kind, but she worried more about her own three children and the one she and Jamie's father had had together. Jamie wasn't neglected, but there wasn't much space for him in anyone's life, either.

Lay the Table and Wait

Jamie's needs were too big for an individual teacher, or even an entire school community, to meet. What's more, Jamie wasn't running toward anything else. He was the happy panda. He was content to be exactly who he was.

For the better, Jamie spent more and more time in secure detention. There he got an education. He also developed his skills as a criminal, but he was doing that well enough on his own long before he crossed through the double magnet-locking doors of his living unit. We all held our breath. His father just shook his head and visited when he could. His teachers by this point had passed him on to junior high, hoping Jamie could make a new start there. There simply was no easy alternative.

Jamie's story may seem a strange one with which to introduce a book on helping adolescents find powerful identities that bring them resilience. But it is a realistic one. Quite frankly, time was on the side of the adults in Jamie's life. Eventually, kids like Jamie come to want more. The older ones tell me as much. What we offer such adolescents is the safety and continuity of a community of concerned adults, even if those adults and that security come in the form of secure detention. The panda, we must remember, eats only one special bamboo. When we offer a 50-foot buffet dinner, it is unlikely the panda is going to pay much attention to our entreaties to "Please eat"—at least for the moment.

Resilience is as much about the structures we create around young people as their individual capacities. Some kids will not immediately choose the alternative identities we offer them. Nonetheless, we must continue to put in place the structures that provide them opportunities to flourish. Resilience is about much more than personal characteristics. Our role as educators and parents is to make sure the table is laid when Jamie gets hungry. In the meantime, we wait.

2

Three Identities

Pandas, Chameleons, and Leopards

Giant panda: A rare bearlike mammal with characteristic black and white markings, *Ailuropoda melanoleuca*, native to a few mountainous areas of forest in China and Tibet and feeding almost exclusively on bamboo shoots and roots.
—*Oxford English Dictionary*

A program I ran through the YMCA in downtown Montréal was meant to offer street kids new identities. However, I think I changed my understanding of the identities those kids had much more than they ever changed anything about themselves. Through my work I found something redeeming to say even about the skinheads from the St. Henri and Atwater districts. There, kids frequently grow up confronting violence and poverty, prejudice, and a lack of access to services. These were creative kids nonetheless: punkers, vandals, and bullies lacking much parental control, frequently on the verge of dropping out of school, but always full of piss and vinegar. I liked them despite the threat they posed to others. I also believed they could change. And they could and did change—only not always in the ways I predicted.

I was hired by the YMCA to draw them off the streets and into activities that were creative and helpful and that met the Y's mandate for social justice. Those wild teens, however, brought themselves and all their deviant ways into the drop-in center. Why would I have expected differently? They laid lines of lighter fluid down hallways and made a blazing trail that almost set off the sprinklers. They both teased me and threatened me, one at one point grabbing me by the collar and lifting me off the ground, reminding me not to be too critical or demanding.

But despite it all, they never hurt anyone, least of all me. In their own way, they appreciated the new audience that we at the Y provided them, and they were more than willing to perform their life stories in front of us with gusto. They entertained staff with stories of stink bombs and suspicious sexual exploits. They blew in and out, all the while searching for something. I think some found it. That something may have been an elusive attachment to someone who looked at them as other than worthless or violent. I may not have always agreed with how they expressed their individuality, but I found myself respecting their inventive capacities to create something from nothing.

If I liked their spark it was because I could identify with it. I understood that many felt stuck with very *thin* descriptions of themselves. They just couldn't say much about themselves that didn't have to do with how they acted when out on the street. Though they were surely more than just bad kids with street identities, those were all the words they had to talk about themselves. I saw in them, though, a keen desire to flex, to be known in more ways. Isolated in their street-smart patterns of behavior, they were headed to extinction as surely as the great pandas of China.

The Stuck Panda

It is no surprise that many of the high-risk youth that most resist changing their behaviors are also those who have committed themselves to one way of living. They have only one identity that brings with it the success they need to feel powerful. I meet many of these youth in my clinical practice. They explain to me their rationale for remaining stuck. It's not that they can't change, they say, it is that frequently their families, schools, communities, and the professionals who try to help offer them *no other more powerful identity.*

Describing themselves as pandas was my suggestion. The youth themselves use the phrase "being stuck." But they don't mind, they even laugh, when I draw their attention to the similarities they have with those big, rather dangerous and unadaptable giants of the Asian forest.

Of course, no child is really a panda. The label is simply an attempt to shake us out of our diagnostic complacency that sees certain kids with certain behaviors in certain (usually negative) ways. A panda, or for that matter, a chameleon or leopard, is neither good nor bad in and of itself. Pandas are who they are. To other pandas, the big lumbering beast that won't change is all one could hope to be. It is we outsiders, those not of the species, who make judgments.

Recognizing the Panda

You can recognize when an adolescent is stuck, pandalike, in the hazy security of a single narrow self-definition:

- The youth repeats behaviors over and over again, even though it appears to outsiders that the youth's problems keep getting worse.
- The youth is seldom interested in opportunities to change, preferring to stay with the same peer group both at school and at home.
- People around the young person see the youth in one way and one way only.
- Despite problems, the youth is likely to say he or she doesn't mind how things are. The young person even impresses others with his or her self-esteem, confidence, and creativity.
- The teenager's patterns of behavior are often self-destructive.
- The teen is good at manipulating teachers and others at school to do what he or she wants them to do.
- The youth has little respect for teachers or other authority figures and doesn't believe that any adult can offer help that provides a better self-description.
- The young person can be dangerous when his or her identity is challenged or put down.

For the panda, life is predictable. We can think of their lives as one long-running performance that travels city to city, playing the same show over and over. Of course, many artists make a fine living doing this. Others, though, prefer to change, adding new voices and seeking new influences for their music. Joni Mitchell has made a name for herself doing just this. In the 1960s she seemed to give voice to the folk wisdom of a generation. I love the old Joni, but I'm inspired that she has demanded of her followers that they grow along with her. *Mingus* drew us to her inspiration in jazz. *Hejera,* a mystical, melodic soulful collection of songs, left behind all vestiges of pop. Joni could have made out very well recycling the familiar, but unlike pandas, she opted not to.

We Find What We Expect to Find

When I encounter people who are stuck, I'm reminded of a Chinese fable:

A traveler arrives at a village and inquires of the people there if their community would be a good place to settle. Meeting an elderly man and his son, the traveler asks, "Excuse me sir, but what are people like here?"

"That is difficult to say," replies the elderly man. "What were the people like where you come from?"

The traveler answers quickly, eager to share his story. "They were mean and selfish, always quick to judge their neighbors. That is why I decided to leave and settle elsewhere."

"That is unfortunate," the old man sighs. "You will find people here much the same. You will need to continue your search." With that the stranger takes his leave.

A month later the old man and his son are at work in their field when another stranger approaches them. He too is looking for a place to settle. Again the old man asks him what his last community was like.

"It was a beautiful place where people helped each other, where there was always time to visit, and where people shared their good fortune with one another. I'd never have left if it wasn't for a drought that has destroyed our crops."

"I think you will like it here," says the old man. "People here are much the same. Come to my house later, and I will introduce you to others who live nearby."

When the stranger had thanked the old man and carried on into the village, the old man's son shared his confusion with his father.

"To one stranger, you said our village is unfriendly; to the other, that we are welcoming and kind. How can this be so?"

"It is not our village that is one way or the other. We have kind people and those who are unkind. The stranger will find exactly what he seeks, wherever he goes."

So it is with Pandas. While those they encounter may or may not react to them in ways that cast them as troubled youth, we must remember that young people exercise some say over how others see them. Those that present an angry front to us and expect us to respond in kind frequently feel justified that their world is, as it seems to them, a cold and unwelcoming place. Only when the pandalike qualities of adolescents are challenged, and new ways of interacting with others introduced, does there exist the potential for adolescents to see themselves differently, and more important, be seen by others differently as well.

Conditions Change, but Not Pandas

The lives of pandas make it clear that all our youth are looking for the same thing. When choices are few, pandas feel most acutely their lack of support, either from their families or communities. They don't adapt easily and are seldom able to move on and find what they need elsewhere. It's far better, they reason, to stay put and perfect the art of whatever has sustained them already through life. It can be difficult to budge them, to make them open to even hearing about new possibilities.

Evidently, neither Geoffrey (the young "bully" I introduced in the first chapter) nor I were truly pandas. After all, Geoffrey could change; he could adapt ever so little in how he related to me. He may not have had many options, but at least he knew that if he wasn't standing on my shoulders to make himself feel important, he could ignore me entirely.

> We can either offer youth who are stuck alternatives that bring with them as much status as their self-crafted way has or we can shape the environment around these youth to offer them as much security and as many predictable relationships as we can manage. Either way, the pandalike teenager gets what he or she needs: the security of knowing that his or her chosen identity works.

More likely, conditions change (they advance a grade), and new demands are placed on youth who must adapt, at the very least carrying their panda identity from one chaotic situation to the next. It is like watching a young child trying to force a square peg into a round hole over and over again. Pandas do well what pandas do, but stress them, and their coping strategy becomes less and less adaptive.

These adolescents are definitely not candidates for home decorating shows where one family hands over decisions to another family and both then enter each other's homes and decorate. Ironically, that is just what many pandalike kids experience, often being the ones who talk of teachers coming and going in their lives, of constantly changing schools because of family breakdowns or because of apprehensions by Children's Aid workers who must intervene when children's behavior is beyond their family's capacity to cope. Suddenly pandas find themselves in new places with new rules. Typically, they cope by playing the same role in the new placement that they played so well in the old. This does not mean pandas will necessarily refuse being placed in new situations. Sometimes pandas just find it easier to go with the flow, to accept life as it is handed them and play out their same part in whatever classroom or family they find themselves in.

Janice

Janice, an 11-year-old, is known as a thief by her family, her teachers, and those in her neighborhood. She hasn't stolen anything much since she was six, when she managed to sneak into a corner store across from her school every day at lunch for weeks, stuffing her coat full of treats. It was a remarkable feat for so young a child. Her friends at school soon encouraged her. The girl's mother, Karen, was busy both at work and keeping her household running and was happy to see her daughter with so many friends when she picked Janice up from the afterschool program she attended so grudgingly.

Karen had her own problems coping with Janice's father, who was frequently absent or emotionally abusive when he was home. An accounts manager at a large bank, he contributed little to the care of his daughter.

When Janice was caught for the *fourth* time and brought back to school by the owner of the corner store, Karen knew her daughter had a problem. To Karen's credit, she kept a much closer watch over Janice and worked with the school playground monitors to do the same. Soon, however, the friends Janice had made began to drift away. Worse, she found that as schoolwork became more difficult, she did less and less well. Janice couldn't read as well as the other children and only just got by in math. It surprised her mother that the smart little girl who had figured out how to steal so much candy was doing so poorly in her studies.

Now Janice's parents argue about her problems. Somehow the stealing episode overshadows all the other challenges Janice faces. It it's perhaps easier to think about Janice as the "thief" than as a child coping with put-downs at home, two arguing parents, or the social stigma of being an outcast at school. If Janice comes home with anything that isn't hers, it is immediately suspected that she has stolen it. Janice, meanwhile, is becoming more and more depressed.

When I met 11-year-old Janice, she insisted she hadn't stolen anything for a *very* long time. Instead, she told a story of living with two parents who often fought and how the brunt of their anger with each other was directed at her.

The real trouble was that Janice just couldn't get anyone to accept her as anything but a thief. She had no other way to impress people anyway. It's no surprise that the only solution she could think of to combat the feelings of worthlessness that she felt was to once again steal. She'd thought about it; she'd even gone into stores and rehearsed what she would do. But she had backed out of taking anything very expensive and so far had only, in her words, "practiced stealing" by taking things like chocolate bars and candy.

She wasn't afraid of the consequences. No way. There would be a lot of good things that would happen if she was caught. She'd get revenge on her parents, and maybe their problems would be noticed. She'd make more friends with what she stole, at least until she got caught. And even then, getting caught would bring with it some status. Time in jail would maybe make her special, she told me. Some of her friends had older siblings who had been incarcerated. They told stories that made the other kids look up to them. Janice was thinking this might be her way out of her depression.

In many ways Janice is typical of most teens who act like pandas. She is stuck with one identity that is thrust upon her by others and that she finds comfortable to sustain. But Janice also knows that this one identity is not going to take her far. She would rather have become something else besides a thief. The trouble was—what? Until that question got answered, Janice was at risk of becoming what everyone thought she already was.

Weathering the Storm

Being a panda, of course, is not all bad. In fact, pandas can be great allies during particularly difficult times. They hold the same course no matter what happens. When chaos finds them, they prove remarkably adept at staying true to themselves. They just aren't all that creative.

In my experience, pandas don't attempt suicide. They persist with patterns of behavior already deeply entrenched. They also don't suffer the angst that plagues many youth who want to change themselves as frequently as they want to change clothes. These young people are ready to hold their course, no matter what the consequences at school or at home.

When the behaviors of pandas *are* fortunate enough to be socially acceptable, these kids excel. They are the obsessive ones who do their homework or who have one hobby that they pursue at the expense of being well-rounded. These are the teenagers who sit for hours by the computer. They are the ones who navigate their way through all the levels of the latest first-person-shooter video games. They carve out a status among their peers as the one who can do one thing well. When that one thing brings them fame and doesn't ruffle anyone's feathers, we generally applaud them.

The good things, then, about pandas include

- Sticking with tasks that say something about them
- Using well-developed ways of coping during times of chaos and change
- Being known to others by one special talent

- A general security and confidence that they do one thing well, reducing the likelihood of depression and suicide
- Predictability

Pandas like these, however, are still very much like those who are acting out in socially unacceptable ways. Both are limited in their choices. The security and predictability they find is as much a noose around their necks as the jailer's key to their freedom. For these kids, Dr. Seuss' *Oh the Places You'll Go* is a nightmare rather than an inspirational tale of a child's untapped potential. For them, it threatens the very foundation upon which they've groomed themselves to succeed. Frankly, they are unsure if they *want* to go anywhere other than where they already are.

PANDAS

➤ Pandas survive by reinforcing one powerful self-definition in all parts of their lives.
➤ Pandas can be very good at accommodating to new situations; they just ignore demands on them to change.
➤ Panda identities depend on others who will keep the panda's identity story strong.

The Places You'll Maybe Go

Sometimes, somewhere along the way, pandas become so secure, or just as likely so bored, with the identity they perform over and over again that they take a risk. Usually, an opportunity arises and, unlike their namesake, these youth take a chance and try something totally new at the buffet that life provides. It takes a combination of a secure environment and access to opportunities for pandas to make this leap.

Any change, especially change that demands a teen find a new kind of story about himself or herself, is met with anxiety. A new story can threaten the old one. Why change, the young person reasons, when invited to do so by a caring teacher, a counselor who is aware of the teen's pandalike nature, or a parent who has the time to listen and understand? These teenagers still find the old more comfortable than the new.

Any new story the youth is offered and expected to experiment with has to bring with it as much, and likely more, power and respect than the story that has sustained the teen all along. At that point of decision, pandas are more like chameleons, that strange lizard that can change the color of its skin to camouflage itself in different environments.

> It is seldom the case that a teenager's behavior, good, bad, or otherwise, doesn't work well somewhere in his or her life. Teachers and counselors need to see how and when the problem behavior works or worked to the teen's benefit. The trick is offering the adolescent who is being asked to change schools, families, peer groups, or communities another behavior that the teen will be just as good at but that fits better with new people and places and the expectations that come with each.

The Uncertain Chameleon

Adolescents who are chameleonlike are adept at fitting with other's expectations of them. They float easily between groups of peers at school, playing the rebel here, the activist there, even the smart or artsy kid when it's appropriate. They impress others with their adeptness in learning the skills needed for each role. They also impress others with how lost they can feel flitting from one identity to another.

CHAMELEONS

➢ Chameleons fit in and adapt their identities according to those they choose to spend time with.
➢ Chameleons choose relationships that allow them to share the power and prestige of others.
➢ Chameleons pride themselves on their skill in creating new identities as they seek out and encounter new people.

Keith

Keith is a young man, 18 years old, who was removed along with his two younger sisters from his mother, Carmen, when he was 11. Carmen's sister called Child and Family Services to report that Carmen was using drugs heavily and badly neglecting her children. The children had to scrounge meals with friends or sleep at other people's homes to avoid the violence, filth, and late-night parties at home.

Though the children were initially all placed together, they were sent to separate foster homes when the girls' behavior became so out of control that they could not be handled by one foster family. Keith suffered through a remarkable number of placements before his 16th birthday. He had five foster homes and as many as eight social workers or case aids that were responsible for him during that five-year period.

Those who knew him during that time say he was very adept at negotiating with those around him for what he needed. He insisted that he be kept in the same school where he knew other children, no matter where he went to live. He maintained reasonably good grades. He attended regularly scheduled visits with his mother. He even wrote to his father, though he never received a reply. And he participated in a number of extracurricular activities, like football and the photography club.

Just before he turned 16, Keith was placed with his last foster family and has lived there since. From the outside it looked as if Keith was a survivor, one of those few young people who manage to rise above the chaos he'd experienced. That was until his 12-year-old foster brother found Keith hanging from the ceiling in his room, his face blue, his body limp and unconscious. Paramedics were able to revive Keith. He says that when he woke up he remembers feeling strangely pleased, though immediately afterwards anxious about what people would say about what he'd done.

Keith's life story might be inspiring if not for the episode that brought him to counseling.

All Keith would say about the suicide attempt was that he was upset that his foster parents hadn't given him the money he needed to join his friends on an overnight school ski trip that had happened two weeks earlier. He'd been too embarrassed to ask his teachers for help.

Keith was sorry that he'd frightened his foster brother but explained, "I felt I had no other choice." Keith got out of the hospital a few weeks later and, wearing a turtleneck to hide his scar, returned to school shortly afterwards. He seemed on the outside to be perfectly adjusted, and it seemed that the suicide attempt had been nothing more than a case of bad judgment.

There is much to admire in a kid like Keith. His adaptability is his greatest strength. But it comes at a price. Not going on the school ski trip was one too many experiences of feeling excluded. Something about that particular episode made Keith feel he wasn't like the other boys. Something in his mind made him think that others were no longer going to let him fit in with them. He not only felt embarrassed about being a foster child, but he also felt *different* from those around him.

Recognizing the Chameleon

We can recognize a youth who is a chameleon when we see patterns of behavior typical of youth like Keith who want to fit in with others at any cost.

- They try on lots of new identities, frequently changing hairstyles, clothes, and peer groups.
- They are crowd pleasers, acting like friends to borrow the status others have.
- They may also like to please adults, wanting to be accepted by doing what is expected, even when they don't agree with what is being asked.
- They suffer greatly with any loss of face, any instance where they have to stand up and be counted in a way that threatens their being accepted by everyone.
- They are the most likely to suffer emotional wounds of rejection and can be suicidal or self-destructive when they fail to get attention from others.

Playing the chameleon is a wonderful launching pad for gaining an awareness that youth want and need to be more assertive of who they are and what they believe. In fact, there are plenty of good things to say about chameleons:

- They adapt well when new demands are placed on them.
- They are comfortable fitting in during awkward social situations and are adept at reading other people's cues about what is expected.
- They are easy to be with and can follow directions well.
- They avoid situations that put them too much at risk, ever aware of behavior in one sphere of their lives that might threaten the respect they get elsewhere.
- They make friends easily.
- They are great shoppers, knowing how to pick and choose the right things to make others see them in the *right* way.

When Chameleons Stop Changing

For many of the youth with whom I work, growing out of their role as a chameleon comes when they encounter a crisis that tears them between two choices. They can continue drifting between identities or stake their reputation on a moment of resistance, insisting others for once accept them for how they want to be known. I often think of one of the boys who taught me this best.

There came a moment for that young man when his friend was about to burn down their school. The boys had both broken into the building one night, and there, with oily rags and a gas can, they were ready to show their teachers what they really thought about being students. Though he was later caught for breaking into the school and doing some minor vandalism, he told me about how he paused and, in that moment of awareness, recognized that he could go no further.

He didn't want people liking him if that was what it took to fit in. When he had backed out, his friend had teased him, but he too had decided against lighting the fire.

> Chameleons will stop changing when they encounter a moral crisis. At some point, adaptation is soul killing, the demands of others too much for them to accommodate. We need to ask chameleonlike adolescents about these moments of decision, to find out how, at times, they make themselves different from others.

It is at such moments, when we discover our moral limits, that we grow, finding in ourselves a new identity as leopards.

The Demanding Leopard

The leopard, youth tell me, finds a way not just to drift between groups like the chameleon but also to be adept at enticing others to accept his or her self-description. "I am . . . " the kid shouts, with enough of an arsenal of tricks to get noticed in different ways by different people, both at school and at home. If I ever need a peer mediator, a negotiator between staff and students, a representative from the student body for the Parent-Teacher Association, or for that matter, a marriage counselor for a family in crisis, I look for the closest leopard.

> Leopards command our respect, even if we disagree with how they express themselves. They are only satisfied when they have convinced others that how they see themselves is the way others must as well. They are assertive and forthright, all qualities we admire in youth who survive and thrive.

Youth with leopardlike qualities force us to accept them for how they want to be known. They are comfortable with us having it our way when it's about us, but they want it their way when it comes to their lives.

Often you can pick out a leopard by the way he or she handles gender roles. They covet their freedom to choose their identity. There are boys, for example, who don't want to be gunslingers, boys who value relationships, and boys who are proud of their artistic abilities. There is a wonderful Irish film, *Billy Elliot,* about a young lad who wants to become a ballet dancer. He completely befuddles his family, especially his working-class father. There is no avoiding being moved by the story. There is something in us that lets us admire the raw, youthful spirit of the teenager who demands others to be supportive in ways meaningful to that teen. That's spunk. It even sells, no doubt because it is inside us all.

Recognizing the Leopard

However, just because we can sit here now and admire these plucky stories of resilience, the truth is that leopards often appear to us like uncaged wild animals that need to be tamed. We seldom embrace them until they have fought pitched battles for our recognition and finally our respect and tolerance. One knows leopards when one sees them. In general,

- They resist conventional dress or behavior and insist on standing out.
- They are unnervingly self-assured, so much so that we are likely to think they are reckless or irresponsible.
- They sneak around, do things behind their teachers' backs, take on new identities, and then insist the school community accept it all.
- They frighten their teachers and others with their forthrightness, their special ways of being whoever they want to be.
- They are fierce and at times unreasonable defenders of others whom they think are being mistreated in their school or in the community beyond.

Distinguishing Leopards From Pandas

It can be difficult to tell a leopard from a panda. Depending on what we think about the leopard's choice of identity, we may think the youth is simply stuck in an old pattern and will grow out of it, when in fact the young person's stubbornness is his or her way of forcing teachers and others in positions of authority to change.

Educating a leopard is very different from educating a panda.

The panda says to adults, "I am what I am. Don't ask me to change. I know you will see me only in one way, but I can't change your opinion of me, nor will I change how I behave! This is the way I know best to survive."

The leopard says something similar but profoundly different. "I am what I am. Don't ask me to change. I know you will see me only in one way, *but I will do everything in my power to persuade you to change your opinion of me.* I will not change myself *unless I find another way of being me that is more powerful. Who I am is my choice to make.* This is the way I know best to survive."

It is this empowered aspect of the leopard's personality that brings with it many impressive characteristics. Leopards are

- Fiercely loyal once they are accepted
- Typically creative thinkers, even if they don't always perform well in conventional roles, like student or dutiful child
- Confident in displaying the talents they have, ready to stand up in assemblies or strut their stuff on the gym floor
- Comfortable with themselves and don't need to put others down to make themselves feel good
- Appreciative when others accord them the same respect they show and will advocate for those who respect them
- Quick to challenge teachers' complacent understanding of what is and is not a "good" kid

Unfortunately, you can find leopards in jails and on the street as easily as in afterschool activities and living at home with their parents. A leopard, like a panda or chameleon, who comes from a tough background will exploit whatever opportunities are available to find a powerful identity.

Shelagh

The first thing you notice about 15-year-old Shelagh is her jet black hair that hangs down across her face. She combs it straight down and lets it shade her eyes. The second thing you notice is that she's thin, very thin, in the way of evidently anorexic young women who teeter on the brink of starvation.

Shelagh had her first encounter with mental health counselors when she was nine. Growing up in a family where her mother was always close to exploding and her father emotionally distant, Shelagh began at a young age to take her own anger out on animals. She'd tie up her cat by its neck and leave it in the forest behind her house for hours, checking back now and again to watch it chew through the cord. She'd catch mice in boxes and chop off their tails or pull legs off spiders. Her classmates at school thought she was weird. Most of them stayed away.

When she did play with other children, she'd play rough, sometimes knocking them down on the playground, always making it look like an accident. Her mother would notice, yell at her some more, and call her names. But that's as far as it would go. People cut Shelagh quite a lot of slack. Those close to her know she has diabetes. For her, it feels like a death sentence. She thinks a lot about the risks she faces: losing limbs, a short life, constant treatment, injections.

Her anorexia doesn't help. She infuriates her teachers and her mother with her refusal to eat lunch and the periodic episodes of insulin shock she has both at school and at home. She refuses to take care of herself. Or so it seems.

She stopped going to school regularly at age 12. She was bored out of her mind. She likes to hang out with only a few other girls her own age. Mostly, she hangs out with older guys, has the label of being "sexually promiscuous," and is rumored to have been trading sex for drugs and a place to crash for nights she doesn't come home. Her school counselor is worried that Shelagh is falling in with a crowd known to recruit young women as dancers for strip clubs.

Everyone is worried about Shelagh—except Shelagh.

The story that Shelagh tells about herself is of a free-thinking, independent young woman whom people haven't taken the time to hear. She likes the way she looks. She couldn't "give a f____" what people think of how she wears her hair or if she passes out occasionally from lack of food. She is not trying to kill herself, she says. She is actually quite enthusiastic about the music she likes, her gothic dress, her interest in the occult, and even her body. She likes being sexually active. Her only problems, she says, are those laid on her by others.

An Unconventional Leopard

A leopard? Maybe, though she's not the conventional leopard we like to meet, not the resilient kid who fits in with our expectations. But a leopard, yes. Here is an "in-your-face" kid who is taking control over her body and her mind and telling people around her to "get with the program."

Shelagh is not likely to give up her stake in her personhood until others give up theirs. She would rather feel alive and in control than the victim of her diabetes. She'd rather look how she wants to look than have others tell her what's healthy. She doesn't care about others' definitions of health. For her, it's all about feeling good her own way.

To get Shelagh to change, and change she must if she is going to see her 18th birthday, we are going to have to understand Shelagh on her terms. We are going to have to offer her something to say about herself as viable as the identity she now carries. "The diabetic," "the good kid," and "normal" are simply not going to entice Shelagh away from her self-destructive behaviors.

As I explain in the chapters that follow, we need to find health resources for children like Shelagh. For example, I wonder if she would have agreed to be the poster child for how children can still live normal lives and have diabetes. Her raging is inspiring, if we choose to look at it that way. Sometimes, when youth like Shelagh are given soapboxes to proclaim their truth, they can be remarkably levelheaded in their advice to others. In my experience, they are the ones who will tell other kids, "Be yourself." Along the way, they seem to get more connected to surviving longer term. They decide they can both be trailblazers and conform enough to medical treatment to secure their own future.

But it is balancing act. A teen like Shelagh needs to know her cooperation is on her terms. That's a hard sell when teachers and parents are worried and a child is in danger. We tend to want to rush in, to save the child, winning a battle but ultimately losing the war when the youth abandons our schools, hospitals, and homes for the street.

LEOPARDS

> ➤ Leopards convince others to accept them as they want to be known.
> ➤ Leopards challenge us to think differently about gender roles, roles related to age, and any other arbitrary way we stereotype children.
> ➤ Leopards force others to redefine what it means to be a healthy child.

Pegs and Holes

It's as if some youth try to be square pegs in round holes, while others survive by happily being round pegs in round holes. Both strategies work just fine in the right circumstances. Like trees, young people either adapt or stand out, survive tenaciously or hide in the shadows waiting to sprout. Each strategy brings with it different rewards. Each suits different kinds of youth. Generally speaking, though, the more youth learn to fit in and be accepted for how they want to be known, the more likely they are to be resilient when problems confront them. Figure 2.1 demonstrates graphically how the three categories of youth go about fitting in.

Pandas are typically those youth who are round pegs in square holes. Notice I say round pegs in square holes, and not square pegs in round holes. The right size of round peg will fit in a square hole even if the fit is poor, the gaps ungainly, and the overall structure wobbly and weak. Pandas are, after all, teenagers who already reside in our communities, whether we want to ignore them, stream them, incarcerate them, or make them into clients of never-ending systems of care and alternative schools. They are made to fit in, no matter how inappropriate the result.

Figure 2.1   Strategies for Fitting In

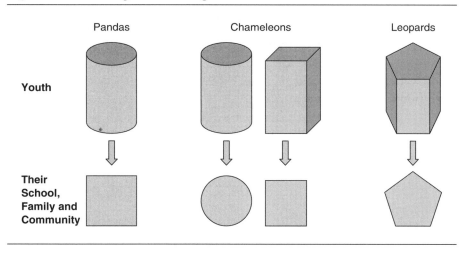

Chameleons, though, have lots of different strategies for fitting in. These are the youth who tried being pandas and chose instead to adapt themselves as often as necessary to fit into many different social situations.

Not so the leopards. They proclaim themselves to be stars and demand that the world shape itself to fit them. Leopards tell me they prefer to altogether reshape the holes they are expected to fit into. They frequently stand out like translucent white birch after a rainfall in a boreal forest.

Listen to Youth to Find the Best Fit

It is exciting working with youth like Shelagh. Though having them in our schools is hell, meeting these kids is like encountering a spring breeze blowing from the south. They invigorate with their spirited defense of who they are. I like to honor that.

Shelagh and her peers are seeking a safe place to be themselves. To the extent that her school provides Shelagh this space, she will respond by attending more.

Our children's adaptation comes disguised in many strange packages. We help young people best when we don't confuse a youth's behavior with the youth's identity. Viewed out of context, any behavior can mean more than one thing.

Dancing on that line between condemnation and acceptance is difficult. It's best accomplished when we, children's educators, are genuine. For example, I encourage teachers and guidance counselors to share stories of their own awkward ways of coping during their teen years as well as accounts of who accepted them and who did not. Youth seem to learn best from us adults when we model for them our own leopardness.

3

Six Strategies for Nurturing Resilience

"Why, Jon, why?" his mother asked. "Why is it so hard to be like the rest of the flock, Jon? Why can't you leave low flying to the pelicans, the albatross? Why don't you eat? Son, you're bone and feathers!"

"I don't mind being bone and feathers, Mom. I just want to know what I can do in the air and what I can't, that's all. I just want to know."

"See here, Jonathan," said his father, not unkindly. "Winter isn't far away. Boats will be few, and the surface fish will be swimming deep. If you must study, then study food, and how to get it. This flying business is all very well, but you can't eat a glide, you know. Don't you forget that the reason you fly is to eat."

Jonathan nodded obediently. For the next few days he tried to behave like the other gulls; he really tried, screeching and fighting with the flock around the piers and fishing boats, diving on scraps of fish and bread. But he couldn't make it work.

It's all so pointless, he thought, deliberately dropping a hard-won anchovy to a hungry old gull chasing him. I could be spending all this time learning to fly. There's so much to learn!

—Richard Bach
Jonathan Livingston Seagull

I f we look back over the stories of youth who survive well, we see some common strategies that educators have used to help nurture resilience in youth who live lives full of risk. Sadly, like that errant parental seagull in Richard Bach's classic tale, *Jonathan Livingston Seagull*, we seldom understand what it is that compels adolescents to be so obstinate in the face of all our good sense!

Overview of the Six Strategies

Over the past few years I have found six strategies that teachers and counselors can use to help high-risk youth and their peer groups construct healthy identities. The sixth and most important, *substitute rather than suppress* (introduced in the first chapter), is the fulcrum point upon which my success as an educator and helper has depended. In family after family, school after school, young people and their teachers and caregivers have taught me that when we offer youth powerful alternatives that bring them every bit as much of those factors they say they need to experience resilience, the more likely they are to succeed. The six strategies are

Strategy 1: Hear their truth—and help them listen for others'.

Ask "What is true for you?" Help adolescents become critical consumers of everyone's values, including those of their teachers, parents, peers, or anyone else who would have them believe their "truth" is *the* truth.

Strategy 2: Help youth look critically at their behavior.

We can help youth understand the benefits they get from both their conventional and unconventional behavior when we show them tolerance and offer open and honest dialogue with them about how their behavior brings with it powerful self-definitions.

Strategy 3: Create opportunities that fit with what youth say they need.

Help youth recognize the challenges they face in creating acceptable and powerful identities because of their gender, race, ethnicity, abilities, sexual orientation, or other structural barriers. Offer opportunities that help them navigate their way around these challenges.

Strategy 4: Speak in ways youth will hear and respect.

Help youth hear what we adults want them to hear by presenting ourselves in ways that do not make teenagers responsible for our fears.

Strategy 5: Find the difference that counts the most.

Help youth identify unique qualities that distinguish them from other kids, especially other youth labeled with problems.

Strategy 6: Substitute rather than suppress (the fulcrum).

As discussed in the first chapter, when we understand adolescents and what they are searching for and how they have created stories about themselves as powerful, we are in the best position possible to offer them what they need in ways that might be less destructive to themselves and others.

When successful, each of these strategies allows us to substitute a powerful pathway to resilience in exchange for the dangerous, delinquent, deviant, and disordered ones many adolescents choose in the absence of other viable and equally powerful choices.

However, these six strategies can't be employed unless there is a relationship between an adult and a teen. There must be association before there can be negotiation. A teenager must be willing to seek help. What we as their teachers and caregivers do makes this more or less likely. Figure 3.1 illustrates graphically what I mean. The six helping strategies, with substitution as the fulcrum, offer a counterweight to the four D's.

Paths to Resilience: Conventional and Unconventional

We have our work cut out for as educators and other concerned adults. As Figure 3.1 shows, how we finesse our way through the implementation of these six strategies determines whether what we offer adolescents is sufficient to pull them away from their unconventional pathways to resilience.

Of course, we do have gravity on our side. Like billiard balls, pandas, chameleons, and leopards are drawn naturally to conventional

Figure 3.1   Conventional and Unconventional Paths to Resilience

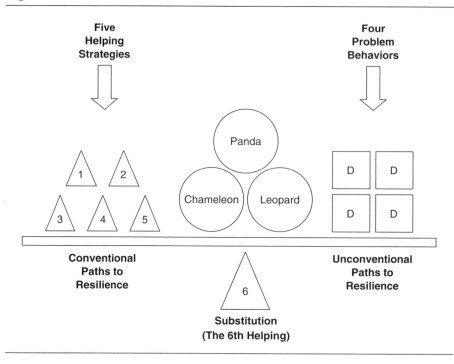

expressions of resilience when such expressions bring both wide acceptance *and* some element of risk.

There is a growing literature on what adolescents need to grow up healthy. Far from security and loving attachments alone, we are learning that youth also need a sense of purpose, rites of passage that help mark their growth from child to adult, equal amounts of risk and adventure sufficient to challenge but not overwhelm, and opportunities to experience both the roots that come with their culture and tolerance for new ways of living (Neill & Heubeck, 1998; Venable, 1997).

The Hidden Coping of Disadvantaged Kids

These six strategies work to the extent that they help us as teachers and counselors develop a new language to describe youth. From a narrative perspective, the language children have to describe their world powerfully circumscribes their experience of it. When we adults help them promote their own vocabulary to explain their experiences of health or offer them useful alternatives that fit with what they perceive as reality, we open opportunities for young people to better understand how they nurture and sustain resilience when faced with risk.

In the first chapter, for example, I discussed my experience being bullied. It is important to remember that I didn't know I was being bullied in seventh grade. I didn't know that I should do anything about it or that anyone could do anything about how I was being treated, at school or at home. Teenagers, I've learned, only name something a problem when they have the words to describe it. The word *bully* would take many years to appear in my dictionary. The word *neglect* would take many more. But in that red brick school building, with the dusty chalk boards and frosted October windows decorated with Halloween ghouls, all I could understand was that I was in Geoffrey's way, that he wanted something I had, and that one way or the other, he was going to take it from me. I'd gladly have given him that which made me more respectable than he, but it wasn't mine to share. I had the talent to do well at school. He was doing his part to survive by showing us what he was good at. He excelled at being bad.

Over the years I've struggled to understand children like Geoffrey. Others have charted these same murky waters. William Pollack (1998), author of *Real Boys*, describes boys as they really are, with far more complexity to their emotional lives than we suspect. Geoffrey is one such boy who needs to be looked at more closely. As Pollack explains, "Though the stereotypes about what boys are and how boys should behave continue to be perpetuated, in our hearts many of us know that these outdated ideas are simply untrue. . . . They often short-circuit our ability to see and love the real boy before us—the true boy behind these old-fashioned ideas" (p. 52).

It's the same for girls. Carol Gilligan (1982) has helped us understand that girls have their own unique ways of making sense of their world and a morality different from that of boys. Mary Pipher (1994), author of the best-seller *Reviving Ophelia*, does a masterful job of filling in the details of how girls find themselves a powerful identity, making rich the lives of girls struggling to express who they are in a world that would rather not notice them.

A Commitment to Survive and Thrive

When children are determined to survive and thrive, they

➤ Make a point of getting through each day feeling a little stronger, a little more in control, and a little more noticed

➤ Follow both conventional and unconventional paths that offer the hope of surviving well

➤ May employ different strategies, depending on whether they are boys or girls, but they express the same needs for a powerful identity and the control that comes with it

Identities That Heal and Hurt

If we mine the stories adolescents tell about themselves, we always find powerful identities. Not all these identities, though, are going to meet with acceptance from those who teach and counsel these youth. For the most disadvantaged of our kids, those who have been neglected, abused, witnesses to violence, or caught in the cross-fire of adult wars, either domestic or those between nations, the identities that help them heal are also frequently ones that trouble us.

Even an adolescent seagull like the one chronicled in Richard Bach's (1970) *Jonathan Livingston Seagull* must resist the advice of his parents if he is to find some way out of the mediocrity of daily survival. How odd that we might expect differently of a boy like Geoffrey. What else could he do that would make him feel as powerful as he does when he plays the bully at school?

Strangely, I remember days wishing the tables were turned and that I was more like Geoffrey and he more like me. Deep down, I knew that I wanted what Geoffrey had: that spark of resistance, the means to fight back better. It was something I wouldn't find on the school yard for some time. And it would be several more years before I learned how to bring it home with me. Even as I was being taunted and hurt, I was watching, learning.

Adolescents need a language to describe their experiences. Without the words to describe abuse, exploitation, and neglect, they are defenseless against those who treat them this way.

Strategy 1
Hear Their Truth

When it comes to hearing an adolescent's truth,

1. Take the time to listen.

2. Keep a positive attitude toward the youth, even if the youth's *behavior* is a problem.

3. Try to understand the world from the youth's point of view.

4. Be curious rather than full of awe and wonder at the stories you may hear.

Listening Well

In the conversation that follows, between a 15-year-old girl and me, all four of the skills I noted in the above box are demonstrated in how I engage her in a structured conversation, one intended to create a relationship, show understanding, and get myself up to speed on how she sees her world and survives.

Bridget

Bridget is from a stable rural family. Her father is a firefighter, and her mother looks after children during the day to supplement the family income. Bridget has a much older brother who has moved away from home. He was never a problem. That's not the case with Bridget.

Her parents struggle with her mouthiness, her truancy, and her outright lies about where she goes and what she does. They still talk with great anxiety about an episode a year earlier when Bridget hadn't returned from school. An anonymous caller had tipped them off to where she was.

They found her in a garage with a dozen other underage youth, drinking. When the parents arrived at 3 a.m., their daughter was drunk but thankfully nothing worse. The gang of them was intending to spend the night. To her credit, Bridget, who was maybe not as drunk as she made herself out to be, actually listened to her father when he ordered her into the car.

Since then, things haven't improved. Bridget's parents don't trust her. Her marks are continuing to slide. Though she visits the guidance counselor almost weekly, their conversations go nowhere. The counselor has told her how she'll have to change, how to handle her parents, and how to stay out of trouble. He's offered support. He's encouraged her. But she just keeps sliding.

A Conversation About the Truth

When the school guidance counselor referred Bridget to me, it looked as if she was about to be kicked out. In the following conversation I do many things, but mostly I am trying to understand Bridget's world. As I listen, she explains to me the differences between herself and her friends. What looks to her parents (and to me as an outsider) like one big, "bad-ass" bunch of truants is actually three groups of kids hanging out alongside one another. In discovering this, I had a choice. I could play cheerleader and encourage her to remain different from her more troubled peers, or I could remain curious and let her tell me why *she had chosen* to distinguish herself as different. I prefer to hold back the applause. I offer only curiosity. The reason is simple: When I get excited about one identity or another, then the teen knows that I will accept her as only one type of person. I foreclose on a youth like Bridget telling me about the other possible ways she could behave.

Her truth is much more complicated. I would rather help her decide what works best. But before I can substitute a different identity story, I need to see behind the facade of the stories we adults tell about her. It's not a surprise that when teachers offer this space— through journal exercises, through lunchtime chats, through any opportunity there is to ask about a young person's life rather than assume we know what a kid's life is like—then we are that much closer to hearing their version of the truth. Our conversation went like this:

Michael (M):   I am curious what you think is going on, what's making it difficult for you to stay at home.

Bridget (B):   Well it's my friends; my parents won't let me hang around with them.

M: What don't they like about your friends?

B: Well, they think my friends do drugs and drink and that I'm automatically going to do it, too.

M: So when you're with your friends, do your parents think they're going to get you into the drinking, the drugs and alcohol? Is that their fear?

B: Well, they think that I'm going to start doing it, a lot of it.

M: How sensible do you think their fear is? Is there a risk?

B: I don't know.

It's no surprise that Bridget responds well to my previous questions then withdraws with the pat "I don't know" we hear so often from teens. After all, my last question all but told her what the *right* answer should be. I catch my mistake, realizing that I am likely missing a whole lot of Bridget's truth if I sit there believing that her behavior and her friends are indeed big problems she has to change.

M: Sorry, I think I may have jumped to some conclusions. Can you tell me a bit more about your friends, what they are really like?

B: It's only a few of my friends doing drugs, but my parents, they think it's all of them. It's mostly the boys.

M: So it's not cool for the girls?

B: Well, not really. I know only two or three who are doing the drugs, and they're all guys.

M: But you are drinking?

B: Yeah.

M: Smoking?

B: No.

M: And how are you doing at school?

B: Good.

M: Hmm, that's interesting because that's usually something that also goes along with being bad.

B: I'm doing good now. I wasn't doing too good last year because that was when there was all the arguing and fighting, and I couldn't really concentrate on it then. But now I'm doing all right.

M: So the school work goes down when the arguing goes up. They are sort of related.

B: Yup.

We talk at this point more about how she used to do at school and what she believes she could accomplish. Far from being a young woman without a positive story to tell, Bridget still holds on to an identity of herself as the "smart and cute" (her words) little girl she was seen as in elementary school. She used to like to read and swim, she tells me, both activities she doesn't do much anymore. She explains why:

M: You said a couple of things you've changed. You don't go to the library, you don't swim. Can you tell me about those changes?

B: Well, once I got into junior high, I began hanging out with my friends.

M: And they don't do those things?

B: No, not really. We like go to the mall or the movies. Or I go for sleepovers.

M: So books aren't a part of it, or you don't go swimming. They're not into it?

B: We would do those things, but we'd rather do other things, like movies.

M: So what about your friends worries your parents?

B: They're just worried I'm going to turn out like a few of my *bad* friends.

M: There's that word again, "bad" friends. *[Bridget laughs.]* What does a bad friend turn out as? What about in school?

B: They do good in school. My parents don't understand that—that they can do drugs but still be good at everything else. And most of us don't even do drugs anyways. But they never think to ask. They don't care that there's only like three groups at the school. There's the preppy group, that are into sports and think a whole lot of themselves, and then there's the library group that would rather sit in the library and read at lunchtime rather than going outside. And then there's my group.

M: How do you describe your group?

B: Not really sure *[she pauses]*. Usually other people say they are the druggies. But that's just like a really strong stereotype. The sports guys are the ones swimming, the library guys are the ones reading, and then there's the druggies. Well, we're mostly all not doing drugs.

M: The way you described yourself in elementary school, I would have plopped you in with a different group.

B: Yeah, the preps probably. Athletic stuff like that. I'm still a bit like that. Like last year I was in cheerleading, and I'm good at gym, though last year I didn't participate in gym because I didn't like the gym teacher.

M: But you were involved in those things.

B: A lot of my friends are. They all participate in gym. But my parents think they are all lazy, that they don't do anything just because they have a reputation for doing drugs.

We talk for another half hour, mostly about her friends and the respect they show her, something she says is in short supply at home.

Eventually, I pull out a pad of paper and a pencil. I want to check with Bridget that I understand what she's telling me. I draw the diagram you see in Figure 3.2. She looks it over and nods. "Yes, that's more like what it's like. We're not all bad, you know."

The Questions Asked

A casual read of the above conversation might leave you wondering which questions to ask and when. If we look back over the sequence of questions, one can observe a pattern.

Figure 3.2   The Groups at Bridget's School

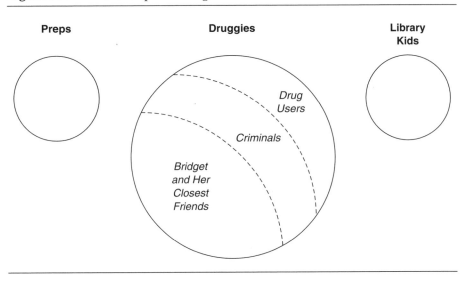

1. I like to begin by *expressing curiosity* rather than judgment, and that includes judgments in the form of applause for behavior that I approve of. That's why I ask questions like, "I am curious what you think is going on, what's making it difficult for you to stay at home."

2. I explore *everyone's perspective* of the problem, not just the young person's. Often this part of our conversation helps the youth give voice to what they know adults are thinking. Remarkably often, teens are very aware of what their teachers' and care-givers' concerns are. However, they have a very different per-spective, or story, to share about how they see their world. It's for this reason that I ask questions like, "So when you're with your friends, do your parents think they're going to get you into the drinking, the drugs and alcohol? Is that their fear?"

3. I *search for differences,* unique perspectives on the problem and its solution that an individual youth, or a group of youth, may have. It is through the discovery of these differences that I find clues about how best to offer a teen a substitute behavior. In Bridget's case, we discovered lots of areas of difference between her and the "druggies" she counts among her peers. All of Bridget's friends are not the same. That's why I asked her if she does drugs, if she smokes, and how well she does at school. It's best not to make any assumptions.

4. I seek to understand why the youth's *behavior makes sense* to him or her. That's why I asked Bridget, "You don't go to the library, and you don't swim? Can you tell me about those changes?" I assume that a youth's behavior has a purpose and that it solves some basic need, even if it looks problematic or self-destructive.

5. I tidy up my language, making sure that the words I use and the words the teen uses mean the same thing. For example, when Bridget tells me her parents call her friends "bad," I don't accept that label at face value. I need to know more. I say, "There's that word again, 'bad' friends. What does a bad friend turn out as?"

These five aspects of my questions avoid creating resistance. These same aspects repeat as I employ all of the six strategies to engage youth in building strengths that are more adaptive in the contexts of where they live. The result is that youth like Bridget have nothing to resist. I'm not trying to convince them that my way is the right way. Instead, I am trying to understand their world from their perspective: their truth. To the extent that I am successful, the more likely they will be to want to work with me on finding better solutions to problems than the ones that are complicating their lives and relationships.

A Postmodern Turn: Kids Constructing Their Own Realities

Who am I to say, given what Bridget has to deal with, that one choice is really better than another? Much of my approach to helping youth like Bridget rests on ideas gaining currency among narrative therapists who have adapted postmodern concepts of truth, knowledge, and power to the helping professions. Postmodernism, a philosophical movement that challenges the empiricism of science as we know it, argues that the world is not a fixed reality but is experienced through the stories we collectively tell about how things ought to be. These collective conversations, or discourses, have been shown by the French philosopher Michel Foucault (1972/1980), among others, to decide for us what is and is not the truth.

Not that all truths are negotiable—far from it. We also hold many truths in common, like our countries' constitutions, like respect for our judiciary, and ideas about what makes us happy. However, when it comes to individual relationships, I am amazed at how often adolescents have shown me how out of touch I am with their realities.

This idea of constructed realities that are fluid and change over time is easily seen when we look back into the recent past and recount stories of adolescents who confided their experiences of sexual abuse to teachers and counselors, only to not be believed because what they were saying was too far beyond the experience of the one hearing it. Today, we might read the possibility of abuse into any experience with a sexual overtone. That change has come about because of the language now available to us to describe our experiences and the power of those who control how we think about sexuality, adolescents, and abuse changing their notion of what is true and not true.

With a new language comes the power to articulate our experiences in a way that privileges our version of reality: no words, no reality!

A youth like Bridget is fighting an uphill battle to get us to understand her truth. Hearing her truth is the first strategy that helps us move adolescents toward healthy and conventional choices for sustaining their well-being.

Fighting the "Loser" Label

Words like *druggie*, *bully*, *victim*, and *survivor* all have definitions that we make up together. Each person we encounter adds his or her meaning to the language we use, and from all the options available, we make a selection of the words that best describe our lives. For many youth, especially those like Geoffrey, whom I introduced the first chapter, this buffet of self-descriptions is sparsely laid. There are few choices for such youth if they are going to be anything more than the "losers" they are already known as in their communities.

And losers they are, at least to outsiders. That word was how a 14-year-old in Taber, Alberta, was known just before he took a shotgun to school and killed one boy and seriously injured another who had taunted him for years ("Loser" kills one, 1999). The boys who were attacked were bullies of a different sort, the preppy, middle-class kids drugged with consumerism, so wrapped up in their worlds of designer labels and the power they have to buy things that they thrash anyone who doesn't "buy in." Losers, kids who don't conform, are a threat to these middle-class "washouts" because they remind the preps how shallow their lives really are.

Finding a Language

Of course, it all depends whose story we hear. It is never as simple as "bad kid brings gun to school." In the back-and-forth negotiation for a language to describe our worlds, we are never passive. But we do take advantage of opportunities as they arise. We move around the world searching for the best description we can find for ourselves. It was no surprise, then, that a 14-year-old took a shotgun to school two weeks after Eric Harris and Dylan Klebold killed twelve classmates and a teacher at Columbine High School in Littleton, Colorado.

Our media handed that unnamed Taber youth the perfect plot line, a different self-description as something other than loser. For other youth, like Emmet Fralick, an East Coast 14-year-old who chose to cope with being bullied through suicide, the solution was sadly just as tragic.

> Youth choose an identity from the options available. *Dangerous, delinquent, deviant,* and *disordered* are self-descriptions that carry a great deal of power for youth whose choices are limited.

Collectively, we decide what words mean. Bridget argues that in her world, the label "druggie" can mean different things from what it means for her teachers and parents. According to her, druggies can still be good students, are respectful of each other, and know how to have fun and take some risks. In her world, the preps are nothing but a bunch of kids too high on themselves for their own good, and the library kids are social misfits.

Is it any wonder, given the choices Bridget perceives, that she chooses to hang out with the druggies? When I stopped to ask her to explain all this to me, in a spirit of curiosity, I was pleased to see her take the time to tell me about the intelligibility of her navigation to groups of kids that help her cope with what she feels are threats to her identity as a happy, healthy, in-control teen. I would not have realized otherwise that all druggies are not created equal but in fact, subdivide into a number of different categories.

4

From Truth to Action

Implementing Strategies Two Through Five

"It's kind of fun to see the expressions the café kids have on their faces when we come to school in these long black dresses. Like when I was walking down the hall wearing this long black dress and this guy said, 'Oh my God, is that a witch?' I started laughing because it kind of feels good to be noticed."

—Jacintha, age 15

Resilience is more than just a set of behaviors or personality traits that we associate with health and successful growth. It is also the ability of children to convince their caregivers that they *are* healthy. Many resilient students are overlooked by their schools and communities because how they survive doesn't conform to what teachers and others in position of authority like young people to be doing. This oversight is ironic. After all, there are many people who have risen to great heights despite the attempted pull back down by those around them.

The video stores are full of movies about them. *Bend It Like Beckam* tells the story of an Indian adolescent growing up in England who is gifted at playing soccer but whose parents refuse to let her play. Breaking with her cultural traditions is her way of resisting the prejudice aimed at her by the wider community. It's the same plot as we find in *October Sky*, the story of a coal miner's son who grows up to be a NASA scientist rather than a miner. One teacher believes in the boy even as the principal of his school and the boy's father do what they can to prevent the boy from fulfilling his potential. And the list goes on.

> Though we might not like the methods young people use to find resilience, we can't ignore the success they achieve through both the conventional, and frequently unconventional, ways they behave.

In this chapter I discuss Strategies 2 through 5, which help us to get it right when we offer high-risk problem youth substitutes for their dangerous, delinquent, deviant, and disordered identities. Each helps us tune in to teenagers' worldviews and examine the barriers to change that they face, and each helps us tailor make powerful alternatives for healthy identities that fit with what youth themselves say they are trying to achieve.

Strategy 2
Help Youth Look Critically at Their Behavior

Youth need adults to help them understand the benefits they derive from both their conventional and unconventional behavior. We help youth when we

1. Show tolerance for adolescents' risk-taking behaviors but offer structures to help keep them safe

2. Ask adolescents how their behavior brings them powerful self-definitions

3. Look realistically at the opportunities teens have to change and remain powerful

4. Change young people's opportunity structures, making new opportunities available that can be substitutes for problem behaviors

A Critical Look

Teenagers' strategies for resilience remind me more of Robert Greene's (2002) *48 Laws of Power* than the kind and gentle wisdom of Mark Victor Hansen and Jack Canfield's (1993) *Chicken Soup for the Soul.* Greene's (2002) sixth law, for example, is "Court attention at all costs." He writes, "Everything is judged by its appearance; what is unseen counts for nothing. Never let yourself get lost in the crowd, then, or buried in oblivion. Stand out. Be conspicuous at all costs. Make yourself a magnet of attention by appearing larger, more colorful, more mysterious than the bland and timid masses" (p. 21).

If I turn to adolescents themselves, I find Greene's (2002) words echoed in their own descriptions of their lives. I have gotten many clues over the past few years about where youth who live lives full of adversity look for health. Health is seldom found where we think it resides.

> When given the chance, youth will help adults understand their lives better. The categories we relish using to sort kids are barriers to understanding them. Wise adults leave narrow diagnoses to those who want to remain smug in their ignorance of young people's truth.

Practice Makes Perfect

Geoffrey (the "bully" who tormented me in seventh grade) and I may have appeared to be on two very different quests for resilience. Indeed, to outsiders, I may have been the one who looked most resilient. Geoffrey would likely have been seen as vulnerable. But that's not how Geoffrey and I would have described our lives. I was seeking the same things as Geoffrey, a way to say something powerful about myself and a creative outlet to express an identity that would be widely accepted by others. Both fortunately and unfortunately, the identity I chose as the "smart" kid brought many rewards—but also many high expectations and anxieties, and it limited the time I spent developing my talents in other areas of my life.

> We adults need to stop making judgments about our teenagers' choices. If we are going to help them find socially acceptable and powerful identities, we need first to understand why their behavior makes sense to them.

Our teens need the space to learn how to negotiate with others for the powerful identities they seek. For example, every new course a student tries comes with the possibility of experimenting with a new identity. If we as their educators and guidance counselors let them experiment with what they want to learn, avoiding a tendency to stream them into what we think is best for them, they may become better and better practiced at convincing others that how they want to be seen is how others should see them.

It is a never-ending negotiation, a dance in which we never quite know who is leading and who is following. After all, how can we say with any certainty what the signs of a healthy kid and an unhealthy kid are? Being judgmental about the mental health of adolescents is difficult to avoid. But the truth, at least according to kids themselves, is that troubled kids may not be as bad as we think. They also may be easier to change than we believe.

Our capacity to overcome incredible barriers in our lives depends as much on the opportunities presented to us as our capacities.

- I had brains (at least with regard to what we studied at school); Geoffrey had brawn.
- I had access to academic success; he had access to the life of a bully.
- We could both change. But it would take a change in circumstances to make that growth happen.

Changing the System While Changing the Kid

When we see the world as our adolescents experience it, we are much more likely to intervene respectfully. Take for example the behavior of students who cut classes. We wrongly attribute all sorts of problems to these students. They must be conduct disordered, delinquent, problem kids, or out of control. All these views are foolish, as least if we listen to researchers who have taken the time to look closer at the phenomenon.

Kirk Fallis and Susan Opotow (2003) have shown us, in their study of kids who skip classes, that the school system may be failing these students as much as the kids are failing the system. In a particularly insightful piece of work, they talk about the incongruity between our adult definitions of boredom and those of students. For students, boredom is something they experience at school when their education is lacking what they need for learning. For many students, there is a deep disappointment with the educational system. Cutting classes becomes a coping mechanism, a way to keep their minds and bodies active when schools fail to engage them.

This is not quite what educators have wanted to hear. We have instead wanted to blame young people, never looking at the assumptions we make that all kids should sit still for hours each day at desks and dutifully learn what we tell them they need to know. Admittedly, if we were to ever abandon our education system altogether and redesign it from the ground up, it is unlikely it would look as it does today. I suspect we would keep kids in school less. We'd return to older patterns of education that emphasized mentorship, apprentice-ships, and community participation. I say this because this is what adolescents themselves hint at when I interview them about their lives at school.

> We have forced our youth to accept the structured and orderly world we adults have created, whether these worlds suit our youth or not. It should not surprise us when they resist.

The Importance of the Questions We Ask

If we are going to ask youth to be self-critical, we should also be open to listening to what they have to say about their lives and the systems that control their lives. An honest exchange of ideas is easier, and can be done without patronizing youth, when we adults under-stand that our role is to model tolerance and teach youth the skills they need in order to be critical consumers of others' truths. Some of the ways I do this are by

- *Showing tolerance* for adolescents' behaviors by asking them about their lives when they are outside school, at home, and in their community. I genuinely want to understand their lives. Most youth, when convinced I'm listening, love to share their stories.
- *Explaining the rules clearly:* Let young people know where the line is that they can't cross, while trying to make the rules unobtrusive and nonconstraining. I am both an advocate for the rights of young people and the one who reminds them of their responsibilities (to get an education, to show empathy for others, to contribute to their family's well-being, etc.).
- Always asking adolescents about the *powerful self-definitions* that come to them because of their behavior and choices, as well as threats to other powerful self-definitions that might come from these same behaviors. Students who get suspended might actually increase their status among peers but at the cost of losing the respect of their parents. Looking critically at one's

suspension means appreciating *both* the positive and negative results of one's behavior.

- Inviting them to join me in looking critically at the opportunities they have to *realistically change* and still feel powerful. I ask them, "What realistically are other ways to feel the same way you do (powerful? happy? attached?) other than getting yourself in trouble?"

Strategy 3
Create Opportunities That Fit With What Youth Say They Need

Youth need adults to recognize the challenges they face in creating acceptable and powerful identities. They need adults to

1. Recognize the barriers youth face in choosing healthy alternatives in resource-poor and dangerous environments

2. Help youth understand the barriers that face them as boys and girls and offer alternatives

3. Make it possible for pandas, chameleons, and leopards to find socially acceptable outlets for their identities

---

Opportunity Structures

Encouraging a critical outlook puts the responsibility back on the shoulders of adults to provide youth options for change. We need to think about young people's opportunity structures, ensuring that there are new opportunities available that can be substitutes for problem behaviors.

I'm no longer surprised by the survival strategies of teenagers like Geoffrey. We've had clues for years that teens make do as best they can with what they have. In 1943, William Whyte published *Street Corner Society*, and suddenly we were able to glimpse inside the ganglike activities of urban communities. What Whyte found, however, seems to have been forgotten. Those young men who lived in Cornerville, the community Whyte studied, understood how their lives worked far better than the outsiders who came to live with them. A boy raised in Cornerville had to either go into the *rackets* (illegal activity) or make his way in *politics* if he was going to succeed.

Those might seem like very different choices—one criminal, the other mainstream and conventional. But that's the outsider speaking.

To those in the community, Whyte (1943) showed, *either* path was a good one. Both created loyalty to the district and brought a high social standing to the young men who participated. The real leaders in Cornerville were not those who gained success outside their community but those who were recognized as leaders within it.

The more we understand, and help adolescents understand, that their choices reflect the opportunity structure that is available to them, the more likely they will be critical of how they behave. One need only think of antismoking campaigns where children are shown how they are being manipulated by Big Tobacco, played for fools by corporate elites, and sold an image that is a falsehood. Tobacco smoking is no longer passively accepted as a way youth address the maturity gap they experience. One way or the other, however, developmentalists like Terrie Moffitt (1997) tell us that children need to find ways to cross this divide between the child and the adult.

Maybe that's why teens have found their own culture, one that includes behaviors that baffle adults: MSN messaging, chat rooms, text messaging, and other forms of cyber communication are one way I see youth finding a powerful identity as grown-up on their terms. Most of us teachers and parents, after all, can hardly keep up with all this newfangled technology, much less program our old VCRs.

And What About the Girls?

Whyte's (1943) work in Cornerville spoke mainly to the realities of males growing up in urban America. Unfortunately, Whyte talks far less about the young women he met. Unlike now, researchers were less interested then in how girls coped with the same risks boys face. In fact, boys and girls often cope in ways that are quite similar, sustaining health through an odd mix of positive and negative behaviors. Only on the surface do the ways boys and girls cope *look* different.

On the downside this means that

- Girls who are exposed to as much stress as boys are just as likely to act out in dangerous or delinquent ways. Both girls and boys who face many different risks are likely to have children earlier, have criminal records, and persist in their delinquent behaviors into adulthood.
- Girls are more likely to be the ones raising the children or tumbling into depression, making them somewhat less visibly at risk than boys who end up breaking the law and going to jail.
- Girls tend to bully almost as often as boys but use covert means, such as taunts, teasing, and excluding other girls from being part of their peer group. Boy bullies tend to use overt behavior: pushing, shoving, and using their physical size to intimidate and control.

- Girls have shown a steady increase in their use of violence as a way of settling arguments. Boys are actually becoming less violent, with an overall drop in violent crime in Western countries.
- Girls now smoke more than boys, using cigarettes as a way to control weight and appetite and convey an image of themselves as mature. Boys are smoking less, though are using more and more body-enhancing drugs to make themselves look a certain way.

On the plus side,

- Both boys and girls report being less sexually active when sex means intercourse (Kids Count, 2004). Boys and girls are, however, as likely as or more likely to experiment sexually, if we think of sex as including oral sex, mutual masturbation, and other forms of sexual contact.
- Girls are now staying in school longer and are more likely than boys to attend university, filling seats even in traditionally male disciplines, such as engineering, physics, and medicine. Boys, meanwhile, are more likely than ever before to become teachers or nurses and to feel less pressure to continue in school or become a family's sole breadwinner.
- Boys are talking about wanting relationships with their children (when they have them). Girls are still confused, however, about how they can manage the dual roles of employee and parent-spouse.

With so much change happening in the way adolescents cope, is it any wonder that we adults are confused? Things are neither as they seem nor as the media would have us believe. Overall, we can say that boys and girls are becoming more and more alike. Sometimes that's good, as when girls pursue higher education. Sometimes it's bad, as when young women take on the violent lifestyles similar to those of the small number of males who harm others physically.

Their choices are reflections of the opportunities available to them. Changes in opportunities for boys and girls have meant more choices for powerful identities. When we as teachers and caregivers provide these opportunities, knocking down walls to equitable treatment of youth, then they have that many more chances to find unique and powerful ways to express themselves through the identities they choose.

How we offer these alternatives and engage with youth in discussions about the choices they have remains a challenge for most adults tasked with reaching out to at-risk children and youth.

Questions to Ask

The best place to start is to think about young people's lives in context. It's reasonable to want our youth to behave in ways we adults find acceptable. It's also unfair to expect this behavior when it makes no sense to the adolescent that he or she should conform. In order to explore opportunities and constraints in young people's lives, I ask them, in one way or another, the following questions:

What would success look like to you? How would you know when you are successful?

What barriers do you face as a [boy][girl][student] to living a successful life?

How does [name the problem behavior like drug use, truancy, bullying] help you succeed?

What are the consequences of this way of achieving success?

Who notices the strategies you use to cope? Do they approve or disapprove? Does either their approval or disapproval matter to you?

In the next chapter, I present a transcript of an actual interview with a boy named Jake that will help illustrate how these kinds of questions are actually formed into meaningful conversations. Strategy 4, meanwhile, provides more specific clues on how to ensure that what we mean to say as parents and teachers is what is heard by the youth in our care.

Strategy 4
Speak in Ways Youth Will Hear and Respect

Youth respond to our questions and hear our concerns when they are confident that we are not threatening their power to decide for themselves how to behave. They need us to

1. Say things in ways that avoid causing resistance

2. Own up to our fears and aversion to risk

3. Offer compassion that is unconditional

4. Model how to express one's truth respectful of others

What Teenagers Hear

Benignly, we adults approach teens inviting them to talk to us about their lives. Often they resist our invitations. So many educators and caregivers tell me that even when they approach teens with honest questions and sincere curiosity, it still feels as if teens close down. Many a teacher and parent have come to me for advice, as if somehow I had a magic wand that could make a teenager speak. If only it were so!

Instead I have to rely on some simple rules of engagement. Here are some examples of what educators and other caregivers say—and what a teenager who is already angry with the adults in his or her life might hear. A teen who has a better relationship with these adults is likely to be less critical, more forgiving. Unfortunately, many of the young people I get to see are far less willing to see the good intentions behind the actions of teachers and caregivers. Here are some examples of the problems that teenagers tell me arise when adults, even well-meaning adults, try to talk with them.

When we say: I want the best for you. I want you to be happy.

The teen hears: I want you to conform, to be just like me. Being happy is living the way I do. What's wrong with that? Let me show you how to do things my way.

When we say: I will try to give you whatever you want. Just tell me what you need.

The teen hears: You need me. You can't get what you need on your own. You are still dependent on me and others like me.

When we say: I'd like to get to know your friends better. Please bring them around any time.

The teen hears: I want to see what you and your friends are doing that might get you in trouble. Introduce me so I can feel useful, an important part of your life.

When we say: School is important. So is going on to college or university. You have to pay attention to your studies. Don't you see that?

The teen hears: You have to grow up and work just like me. You have to have an education, or else you won't amount to anything.

When we say: Your body is your own body. You need to respect it and not let anyone tell you what to do with it that makes you feel uncomfortable.

The teen hears: You have no sexuality. You couldn't possibly handle an intimate relationship. You should wait until you are an adult like me to express yourself sexually. Your body may be yours, but I still want to control what you do with it.

Admittedly, we adults are not going to like the way adolescents hear what we have to say. "Damn it all," we insist, "I have the kid's best interest at heart! If I don't say those things, what do I say?" The problem is that each of those statements needs to be said. Each shows commitment, compassion, and the sincere desire to guide teens into adulthood. And each can be helpful when the young person really believes the adult has the teen's best interest at heart. However, when there is tension in the relationship, a different way of expressing ourselves as adults is needed.

A Different Way of Saying What Needs to Be Said

These other ways of approaching youth recognize that the troubling and dangerous behaviors of adolescents that worry us and that we want to change will change when youth feel respected and heard. If we change what we say as adults, we are much more likely to get a conversation going or at least convey the message that we are there for the youth in our care, should they encounter a crisis. For example,

When we say: It means a lot to me when you are happy. What makes you happy? What about your life is working for you?

The teen hears: I'm comfortable expressing myself. I want to understand your world and how it works. I want to avoid judgment. I don't really know much about your life. I need you to tell me how it works.

When we say: I know you have been good at finding what you need. If there is anything that you need that you still can't find, please let me know, and I'll help you get it.

The teen hears: If you need me I'm there. Tell me how I can help. I know you are competent and can do things for yourself.

When we say: What are your friends like? What's special about them that has made you choose them as your friends? Do you think I'd like them if I met them?

The teen hears: I want to hear about your friends and what in particular you like about them. I want to open up the possibility of meeting them, but you can decide if that's a good idea or not.

When we say: School is important. So is going on to college or university. It's meant a lot in my life getting (or not getting) enough education. Do you have an idea of how going to school, or not going to school, is going to make a difference in your life?

The teen hears: You are growing up and making decisions that have long-term consequences, as they did for me. I have given education a lot of thought and hope you do too. But I also want to understand what education means to you. Is it relevant? Will it make a difference in your life?

When we say: Your body is your own body. It can have lots of different feelings. It's all right to express these. It's okay to have thoughts and feelings that are sexual. I hope you are able to find ways to express yourself in ways that make you feel comfortable. I also want you to know you can come and talk to me if something happens that makes you feel uncomfortable about your body or how others treat you.

The teen hears: You have a sexuality. I know you will express that. I want you to have a positive experience of those thoughts and feelings and feel in control of your body. I'm there to help you if you get into trouble in your relationships.

It is not possible to do more than hint at what we can say to a teen. Every situation begs for new language. Whatever well-intentioned thing an adult says to a young person will be helpful. Adolescents tell me this over and over again. However, in each of the second set of examples, the adult does several things that adolescents tell me make it *easier* to hear what adults are telling them. Adults, be advised:

Don't tell, share.

> The caring teacher or counselor, caregiver or parent doesn't tell the youth what to do but instead offers to share information about the adult's life experience.

Not knowing is a good place to start.

> The adult inquires with sincere interest about the youth's life: what he or she likes and dislikes, feels and thinks.

Favor choice over advice.

> The adult leaves the choice for how the youth behaves up to the youth. It is unlikely the young person will follow the adult's advice anyway, so why sacrifice the relationship for the sake of trying to be authoritative?

Share from the heart.

> The adult owns his or her own feelings and thoughts, explaining what happened in his or her life and the consequences.

Be there, now and forever.

> The caregiver offers to be there when the young person wants to share things about his or her life, but the timing is up to the youth.

When we position ourselves as respectfully curious and appreciative of what the youth is trying to accomplish by his or her behavior, communication is most likely to flourish.

Strategy 5
Find the Difference That Counts the Most

Youth need adults to recognize how they are different from other troubled youth. They need them to

1. Avoid labeling young people unless youth find the labels of use in understanding themselves and their behavior

2. Offer youth unique opportunities to show themselves as powerful and in control of their lives

3. Advocate individualized education and treatment plans for students

4. Nurture "audiences" that are large and varied who can appreciate a young person's performance of a powerful identity that is socially acceptable

Young People's Motivation

Because I think about patterns of resilience in the lives of youth who are burdened with problems, I am more likely to notice how adolescents navigate toward what they need to be healthy. Unfortunately, what I often see is risk-taking behavior that threatens my sense of security. So I clamp down. Instead of understanding teens' motivation to take risks in order to find powerful things they can say about themselves, I hesitate, or insist they pull back.

I overlook what youth tell me. They say they need to do things that make both them and the adults around them uncomfortable if they are going to manage to find acceptance among people they admire.

Labels Hurt

Taking my lead from youth themselves, I resist labeling kids. I realize that our compulsion to diagnose is strong. We find labels and their diagnostic criteria bandied about as often in professional reports as on afternoon talk shows. They have become a dangerous shorthand way that adults refer to youth. They are not benign, though. This psychological discourse defines a young person's life by one single aspect of his or her life story.

Instead, I encourage educators and counselors to notice how students are different from the stereotypes others have about them that constrain their lives. This includes the diagnoses many of them carry that hold kids in the death grip of predictability. I'm not alone. Kenneth Gergen and others have cautioned us that diagnosing behavior, especially among adolescents in the throes of development, serves little purpose for *them* (Gergen, Hoffman, & Anderson, 1996). For we adults, it might reassure us or guide treatment and medication. However, treatment is seldom effective unless the identity that goes along with the diagnosis fits the adolescent's self-definition as still powerful and capable of overcoming life's challenges. For many pandas, chameleons, and leopards, being labeled is simply another excuse to rebel, to complain, "I am not being heard."

I want to find out things about the teenagers I work with that make them unique, powerful, and confident. I want them to explain to me how they achieve feelings associated with resilience.

Bullies Are Kids, Too

After all, a bully like Geoffrey, referred to earlier, is not just a bully with a pattern of behavior associated with an oppositional defiant disorder, attachment disorder, and unrestrained narcissism. He is also the son who must care for a mother when she is tired and hurting from the abuse she has had to endure from a husband who drinks.

The bully is also the victim, ever under surveillance, ever vigilant to the truth others want to lay upon him. These are kids guarded against the fact that they have few prospects for the future, that they are neither bright enough, strong enough, diligent enough, nor loved enough to succeed.

If we put aside the labels, lay down the binoculars that we have been looking through backwards, and appreciate the world momentarily from the point of view of these youth themselves, we learn something about violent youth and about their victims.

It's not an easy place to position ourselves. As Richard Carlson (1997), author of *Don't Sweat the Small Stuff . . . And It's All Small Stuff*, wrote, "Let others be 'right' most of the time" (p. 33). We have to accept that young people take the oddest, sometimes most destructive, paths to health. It has ever been thus.

We can chuckle at our belief that all youth are hell-bent on destroying our culture, on doing things wrong. And Geoffrey, the "bully" who tormented me in Grade 7, was bent on such destruction. But to understand Geoffrey as just a bad kid leaves him no space to tell us how, from his point of view, there is also something "right" about what he does. *If we are going to change Geoffrey (and that is my goal, if only for the sake of Geoffrey's victims), we are going to have to first understand Geoffrey's version of the truth and what it says about his life.* We are going to have to understand Geoffrey as an individual, not one of a category we term "bully." Geoffrey, like all bullies, is still to his mind an individual and as such needs us to appreciate his version of his truth as unique.

Geoffrey's Last Performance

I never spoke with Geoffrey about his behavior. Looking back I can see there was much more going on in that Grade 7 classroom than I understood at the time. Geoffrey really wanted to be the class clown. He just couldn't quite pull it off. That's because there was a girl in our class who was a wisecracking, cussing, angry girl who could as sweetly as could be kick a boy full force in the groin and then smile while stepping over him as he lay on the ground throwing up. Geoffrey, I think, wanted her power. Hers was easier to get than mine. All he had to do to join her team was to be every bit as evil.

Geoffrey became known among the boys for his sexually explicit jokes and his accounts of his older brothers who let him peek while they had sex with girlfriends. He found in the pages of pornography the accounts he needed to shock my pubescent peers. All this made relationships with Geoffrey more complicated. After all, I wasn't the only one who had to steer clear of him.

And yet, though we were trying like small sailing boats in a busy harbor to stay out of Geoffrey's wake, there was something that always pulled us to at least follow him from a distance and listen to his bathroom wisdom.

This strange relationship between Geoffrey and me and the harassment that went with it might have continued for some time if it hadn't been for a strange convergence of events.

It was late November, and lunches were now more frequently eaten indoors in our basement cafeteria. One day, there were french fries, and I'd gotten myself a plate and sat down at the end of one of the folding tables arranged in rows across the parquet tile floor. I had put the glasses I wore into their plastic case, as I always did when I left class. I never liked wearing them. I put my glasses case on my food tray.

Geoffrey came over midway through lunch, giving my tray a good bump, then—turning around laughing—leaned over me and began to eat the fries. He just stood there eating. Not many, but enough to remind me how utterly silly I looked letting him do this to me. There were two or three other boys who had been walking with him when he banged my tray. I could see them now, waiting in line for food but clearly watching Geoffrey.

I got very confused in my embarrassment. My head felt hot; I was blushing red, my thinking clouded. Geoffrey only ate from my plate for a few seconds. Then, with one last shove, he walked away. I wanted so much to say something to him, and then when I said nothing, to leave, quickly. But I couldn't get up, as that would be more embarrassing. It would be to publicly admit he'd desecrated my lunch. So I waited, at least until Geoffrey and the other boys were safely in line for food, their attention on ordering. I got up and dumped my tray and left the cafeteria, found my quiet spot out on the playground and forgot about the cold while I sat there on the school's back steps and tried to calm down. I was close to tears.

When the bell called us back to class, I realized my glasses were missing. This was no small deal. My family didn't have much money, and I had already broken a pair of glasses late the summer before. I'd pleaded with my parents to spend a little extra and buy more fashionable frames, even contributing some of my own birthday money to help with the cost. I feared having to tell my mother about the glasses. But I frankly feared even more having to wear cheap frames that would make me look even more like a geeky "browner" than I already felt.

Evidently upset, I ran to my homeroom teacher and said, "I have to go back to the cafeteria to find my glasses!" Of course, I must have dumped them in the garbage, I thought. Frantic, I ran to the basement and began to rifle through the leftovers of hundreds of lunches. I checked with the cafeteria ladies, and they assured me the garbage hadn't been emptied. Thirty minutes of searching and no luck. By this point I was in tears. And that's when I figured it out. I kept going over and over in my head what could have happened to the glasses. It had to be Geoffrey. It just had to be.

I washed and went back to tell my teacher that I hadn't found them. I knew she knew I'd been crying. I told her I needed to phone home and tell my mom what had happened. She took me down to the office where the guidance counselor was called, and I was invited to phone home from her office. All the while I kept thinking, this is going to be easier if I don't have to explain all of this when I get home.

I was torn, though, whether to take the blame for what had happened or to tell my mother that I was sure Geoffrey had taken my glasses case from my tray. For my own sake, I took the chance and told my mother what by that point I was certain had really happened. Geoffrey had been picking on me for months and likely taken the glasses. The next thing I knew, she was telling me to put the guidance counselor, Mrs. Morrison, on the line. A few minutes later, Mrs. Morrison hung up. She said that she would do what she could to find my glasses. She asked me why I thought Geoffrey had taken them. I explained how he had been treating me. It felt good to drop the burden that I'd been carrying. She nodded. She listened. Best of all, she believed me.

Mrs. Morrison had me wait in her office. She said she was going to speak with Geoffrey. It would take a few minutes, but she wanted me to wait. I said nothing. But I worried what would come next. What was I in for now: trouble at home and more trouble at school? I just sat there, again close to tears, and fidgeted with my shoe laces.

Twenty minutes later Geoffrey and Mrs. Morrison came in to the office where I was still sitting. I put down a book I'd picked up on a shelf next to Mrs. Morrison's desk. Neither Geoffrey nor Mrs. Morrison sat down. Mrs. Morrison asked Geoffrey in front of me if he had taken my glasses.

"No, I didn't do anything," he said.

She gave him a stern look and told him, "Fine. This is serious, though. Enough. The next time you bother this boy, this will go directly to the principal. No more chances. You understand?"

Geoffrey didn't look very big at that moment but sort of flabby, and his eyes were moist. I think he was confused. I'd thought he'd taken the glasses, but looking at him, I felt a little bit ashamed. Maybe he hadn't. It didn't really matter, though. They were clearly gone. My parents would have to buy another pair. I'd be yelled at or worse for not saying anything about Geoffrey earlier.

The Biggest Gain for the Least Pain

Strangely, and this is what confused me most, Geoffrey disappeared from my life after that encounter in the office. He never approached me again. He never hassled me again. In gym class, a particularly awkward place where it was evident that I was a year younger than the other boys, he never teased me. He never pointed in my direction in the shower room, making me ashamed of my body. He let me be invisible. He didn't change, of course. There were other victims. But thankfully, I was no longer one of them.

FINDING AN IDENTITY

> ➢ Identities come to us through language; they are words invested with meaning and power.
>
> ➢ Identities fit with the circumstances of our lives. They reflect our access to whatever we need to make ourselves feel healthy.
>
> ➢ Identities are chosen to make us different from others.
>
> ➢ Identities are "performed" in ways that persuade others to see us in the ways we want to be seen.

Youth take the path to health most readily available. Those that present obstacles are avoided in favor of those that are more easily traveled. The only exception to this rule is when the path less traveled offers special rewards that make it worth the extra effort.

In time, and with the help of conversations with hundreds of other young people, I think I have come to understand better why Geoffrey gave up on me. I was simply no longer worth the effort. Geoffrey never intended to work very hard consolidating a powerful identity. He needed too badly to feel powerful, and frankly, attacking me threatened the likelihood that he was going to survive. If he wanted pain and suffering, he could find that at home. At school he had seized the opportunities available to him to feel every bit as powerful as he could be.

Mrs. Morrison was great. She defended me. She made junior high easier. But she didn't take that next step and offer Geoffrey anything but a roadblock. She never quite understood what Geoffrey needed as an individual or why his behavior made sense to him.

We now thankfully have the means to help students like Geoffrey much better than we did before. The solutions we seek to help such students change are now as close at hand as the youth themselves, when we take the time to listen closely to what they tell us about their lives. The sixth strategy for helping youth, the one I started with in Chapter 1, is also the last one we need to finish with if we are going to make our interventions count: *substitute rather than suppress*. It is the fulcrum upon which a youth's behavior teeters. The five preceding strategies simply set the stage to get this substitution right, to ensure that it fits with how the youth sees his or her world and what he or she needs.

In the following chapters, I explore in greater detail this sixth strategy, providing clues to how we can offer these substitutes by understanding what youth need most and how they make do with the resources they have available.

5

The Many Expressions of Youth Resilience

I'm boiling with rage, and yet I mustn't show it. I'd like to stamp my feet, scream, give Mummy a good shaking, cry, and I don't know what else, because of the horrible words, mocking looks, and accusations which are leveled at me repeatedly every day. . . . I can't let them see the wounds which they have caused, I couldn't bear their sympathy and their kindhearted jokes, it would only make me want to scream all the more. If I talk, everyone thinks I'm showing off; when I'm silent they think I'm ridiculous; rude if I answer, sly if I get a good idea, lazy if I'm tired, selfish if I eat a mouthful more than I should, stupid, cowardly, crafty, etc., etc.

—Anne Frank

Occasionally, teachers and counselors in the throes of crises misunderstand what youth are saying. More to the point, they wonder if accounts by youth that appear to show that dangerous, delinquent, deviant, and disordered behavior helps them survive are all a lot of misguided foolishness. Besides, such behavior makes their jobs as educators and counselors that much more difficult.

I'd wonder the same if I didn't keep hearing even our most troubled youth tell me that they don't think it's OK to do drugs, be abusive, drop out of school, or in any other way harm themselves or others. They know as well as I that being dangerous, delinquent, deviant, or disordered has its drawbacks. But they also know that in the absence of options, these behaviors make sense.

Strategy 6
Substitute Rather Than Suppress

Youth need adults to offer them powerful alternatives to "problem" behaviors. They need adults to

1. See their choices of dangerous, delinquent, deviant, and disordered behavior as coping strategies in under-resourced environments

2. Offer them new and more widely accepted stories to tell about themselves

3. Play the audience to these new stories

Needed: A New Self-Definition

Teachers and concerned caregivers worry that if we acknowledge the reasonableness of young people's behavior, even for a moment, we reinforce it. This is the same fear that drives educators and parents to oppose high-school-based day care for teenage mothers and their babies. "What if my student (daughter) sees those girls with their babies? It will make her want to have one as well!"

Such beliefs are not as rare as one thinks. Remarkably, we believe that a teenager who has options would *choose* the chaotic life of the teenage mother. Of course she would, and we know this from numerous studies, when with the role of teenage mom comes a personal definition as a contributing part of her community or at the very least, recognition as an adult (Ladner, 1971; Taylor, Gilligan, & Sullivan, 1995). The only girls I meet who have children they didn't want are those who got pregnant by accident. For those girls, the role model of the teenage mom at school is much more likely to be a deterrent to unsafe sex, a wake-up call to the consequences of what they are doing. For the others, those that would choose becoming mothers in order to find status, seeing a baby with its mother at school presents a much better option than a mother with a child alone at home: you can be both a mother (and therefore a recognized adult in your community) and educated!

In this chapter I look at many important aspects of our teenagers' resilience. These, they tell me, are the building blocks for success. Adolescents also tell me not to assume that expressions of resilience cannot be found just as easily, and in fact in many cases far more easily, in problem behaviors. In the search for powerful identities, it is best to keep an open mind.

> Our teen's behavior makes more sense when we think back to our own childhoods. We too went searching for powerful identities. For many of us, these expeditions to health led us into strange places that were as disapproved of by our parents as our children's behavior is today.

We know this to be true because it is also our dirty little secret. If we are honest with ourselves, we know that when we were teens, we did things that purposefully put us in harm's way, all the while feeling better about the identity we were carving out for ourselves!

Sam

Lisa and Tom are the parents of a renegade 15-year-old boy named Sam. Sam has threatened them with a knife, stolen from everyone in the family, and disappeared often for days at a time, couch surfing with friends, staying high, avoiding any responsibility. Likewise, he has ignored his parents when they insisted he go to school, just as he's dismissed praise from his teachers that he could make something of himself if he tried.

Lisa and Tom are good parents. Sam's school has gone the extra mile for him as well. Still, nothing has worked to engage Sam in more responsible behavior.

Lisa says, "I'll never give up on Sam," and she means it.

I work with a group of adolescents who are in recovery for drug and alcohol addictions, and I conduct a support group for their parents. That's where I met Lisa and Tom. I was impressed by the spirited support that they and other parents showed for their children. They hadn't given up, though in many cases, they've had every reason to. These young people had physically abused them, stolen from them, damaged their homes, dropped out of school, and embarrassed them in their communities. These parents were the walking wounded, and yet they still came forward, intent on finding a way to keep their kids safe, at home, and in a healthy relationship with them.

There are no easy solutions for teens like Sam. Nothing his parents, teachers, or others say seems to make sense. But Sam, as his parents told me, had—to his credit—come in from the cold. He was in a detox program, getting some schooling, and planning to go home and back to school. The glamour of the life beyond his front door had faded. His parents weren't hopeful that the changes would last. They said they had managed to get him to agree to treatment only when it became apparent to Sam that he was headed into worse trouble. Lisa and Tom figured he had agreed to meet with counselors because it was an easier road to travel than jail time. And that's where Sam was headed. He knew it, and his parents knew it. The lifestyle beyond his front door had meant putting himself more and more in harm's way, stealing for money, trafficking in drugs, doing whatever was asked of him by others. Without an education, there would soon be no other options for him but to pursue more criminal activity.

> Kate
>
> Kate, a teenager, is in detox for abusing pills, ecstasy, and pot. Her parents, Bonnie and Phil, attend the parent support group and listen quietly, at first. Then they get exasperated, and one wonders aloud, "How can these kids who have everything do this stuff to themselves? I don't understand. How can they do this to their parents? Kate has pretty much whatever she wants. Why the drugs? And then the boys, and whatever else. We're sure we haven't heard a 10th of all that she's into."
>
> They probably haven't. It's unlikely that Kate's school counselor or detox therapist know any more, either.

I listened and then tried to explain to the group that kids like *playing at being bad* (Ungar, 2002). It is an appropriate description of teenagers like Sam and Kate. Adolescents seek out, then go to great efforts to maintain, an identity they see as powerful. In the process they negotiate for what they need to say something about themselves they like.

Understanding adolescents as pandas, chameleons, and leopards helps us look more closely at these patterns. Acquiring and keeping a powerful identity as one of those three animals happens in many different ways.

Substitutions for Drug Use

Helping teens say "No" to drugs and moving them to substitute behaviors is not easy. Drugs, any drug, whether crack or caffeine, alcohol or pot, create two levels of addiction: the physical dependency and the psychological need. Detoxing teenagers means first creating holding environments around the young people to help them fight the physical addiction. It means us, their caregivers, teachers and professional helpers, saying "No" for them. It means removing the drugs and alcohol from our homes and playgrounds. It means forcing adolescents into treatment—sometimes more than once. It means getting the teenager safe enough, and clear-headed enough, to begin a dialogue about the *good* things that they found when doing drugs.

Meeting Psychological Needs

After all, it is reasonably simple to help someone break a physical addiction. But it is the psychological needs that are the real challenge. How do we offer Sam and Kate substitutes for the social lives they enjoy using drugs? How do we offer them an alternate peer group? How do we offer them the adventure and risk taking they associate with drugs? And how do we offer them another way to make them feel as if they are adults, in control of decisions that affect their lives? How do we offer them all this when they look to be so vulnerable, so unready to take responsibility—so in need of control?.

Using the Strategies

If we go back to the first five strategies, the answers become a little clearer. First, ask teens what they like about doing drugs. Ask the question with sincerity. Ask the question the same way you would want to be asked when someone asks you why you drive the car you do, why you decorate your home the way you do, why you choose the friends you have. When we understand the social and psychological aspects of addiction, the emotional highs, the energy and spirit many teens like about themselves when high, we are that much closer to knowing what to offer teens as an alternative.

It also opens the door to a conversation that can then become more critical. Are there things about doing drugs that the youth doesn't like? Do we as our children's caregivers and educators offer teenagers the transparency of our own self-criticism, our own self-doubts about whether we feel at times manipulated into doing things we don't want to do? Do we tell them about the hangovers? Are we honest with our kids about the downside of cigarette smoking or caffeine use or other socially acceptable addiction? These conversations model for our youth ways of being self-critical without being critical of them.

Youth tell me they appreciate it when adults understand their drug use as something that opens up opportunities rather than drugs being all about making problems.

All these strategies depend on our speaking with youth in ways they can hear. They don't want lectures. They want compassion, the ability of those who love and care for them to comprehend why they do what they do.

And teens want to be asked how they are different from other teens. Kids who use drugs tell me they pride themselves on being the one among their peers who can (a) use more drugs than any other kid and survive to tell the tale; (b) use drugs wisely, making choices about how much, when, and what drugs are going to be a part of their lives; or (c) be a part of a drug-abusing peer group and not become addicted ("Really, I'm not!" they insist). We adults might guffaw at all three ways kids say they are different, lumping them all together as delusional addicts up to no good—except that's not how our young people see themselves. They distinguish themselves from their peers. They make choices from the limited resources they have.

Substitutes for Sam

For Sam, a substitute behavior would have to bring with it lots of adventure and a healthy dose of control over his life. I was hesitant to recommend Sam slip back into a responsible middle-class lifestyle with the routine of school and a few close friends, sports, maybe a night out at the movies on the weekends. Yawn! I knew that this lifestyle would please Sam's parents and his school. It might even hold Sam's attention in the short term now that he is off the drugs. But long-term, I was worried. Instead, I imagined Sam would be more likely to put the drugs behind him permanently when he felt he had control over his own money and lots of adventure to distract him.

It might seem odd, but I have learned from teens like Sam that they often crave a job. One young man I know works weekends unloading trucks. In the camaraderie of the loading dock, he has found a status among men unavailable to him in school or at home. He also gains the independence that comes with earning his own cash—and the responsibility of knowing he can't do drugs and hold a job at the same time.

This, of course, is just one possible solution. There is no recipe book. The six strategies help to provide the details so that a plan can be hatched, one that when tailor-made for a particular young person like Sam will be successful. After all, one has to appreciate Sam's motivation for doing drugs in the first place, as well as the resources he, his family, school, and community can offer as substitutes.

Substitutes for Kate

It is often difficult for parents who give their children everything to realize that they may have given too much. I'm always intrigued by adolescents like Kate who appear to be screaming for anything but the orderly world of the 'burbs. When I see children from good families in good neighborhoods who are running the roads, risking themselves sexually, and well along their way to a drug addiction, I can't help thinking, "These young people are yelling to us for help."

Kate has everything—except a rite of passage to adulthood, recognition as a sexual being, and a mature place in her community. Her search for all these things has led her to the most accessible alternative, a peer group who is handing her an easy-to-follow script for rebellion.

What we need instead is to offer Kate is *a better way to rebel.* Quite often, I find myself strategizing in conversations with parents of teenagers like Kate. What battles are the parents willing to lose? What freedoms can they offer their child? I encourage them to think of this approach as losing battles to win the war. I also strongly encourage them to create a *box* around their teen: a very large box, with limits and expectations, responsibilities to others and commitments to family that must be fulfilled. But such a box must also still be big enough that the young person can find lots of ways to rebel.

Substitutions for Other At-Risk Behaviors

Let's say a student doesn't want to go to college right out of high school. Then what about a work exchange program outside the country? What if a boy in recovery wants to feel more independent? What about putting him in charge of security at school dances? What about renovating a space in the basement at home so a girl has her own space? She can do her own laundry, cook her own meals, or better, cook for everyone else in the family. It has surprised me the number of times youth have argued with their families to eat *more healthfully,* perhaps vegetarian one day a week, or in some other way become something better that will make them different from their neighbors.

At school, how often is space opened for the participation of the most at-risk youth in the governance of the school? The strategy here is not to abdicate adult roles but instead to dialogue with youth about what they need and to model socially acceptable ways of finding compromise solutions that meet the needs of teens in ways that don't overtax the tolerance of the adults in their lives.

Needless to say, offering good substitutes for our children means starting at home and in our schools, presenting them with opportunities to practice being different in socially acceptable ways, even when those ways annoy the heck out of us, the adults who look after them.

These solutions may seem *too simple* to most educators and parents. Why would any young person be willing to accept such easy substitutions for their reckless lives? It hasn't surprised me that most youth tell me they crave relationships with their parents that are more equitable. They want to be a part of their communities. They want an education and a future. But they want all these things negotiated with them and provided in ways meaningful to them.

They want to be resilient, but they also want to follow their own paths to make it happen.

The Many Expressions of Resilience

At some point during my career, the kids won. I tried my darnedest to convince myself that only some behaviors made sense. Of course Sam and Kate were wrong, entirely wrong, to drift into drugs. Drugs cause more problems than they are worth. I hope I've made it clear that I don't want kids doing drugs! I don't want drugs to be an alternative to growing up and learning the right way to cope with life.

I still hold these beliefs, only I see that they aren't very useful when it comes to counseling, educating, or parenting.

Instead, I see now, with the help of the youth I've worked with, that a constellation of many different factors protect our youth from risk. Even when we can't see the risks they face, kids tell me they can get confused or worried or feel put down in situations I'd never have guessed made them feel that way. That's where creative ways of coping come in. Kids may not always execute beautiful maneuvers when it comes to dealing with life stress, but they do keep looking for powerful identities that bring with them the hope of success.

> Expressions of resilience may not come out smooth and polished. The building blocks of health for the delinquent are frequently the same as those for the young person who succeeds in ways applauded by his or her community. Caution is needed when changing a problem youth. The foundations that previously offered support during times of great need can inadvertently be destroyed.

Many Paths to Survival

In my travels I've met youth who rise far above their adversity in creative ways. In a Palestinian refugee camp, I met boy scouts who not just welcomed me but shouted their greeting at the top of their lungs accompanied by a collective pledge to protect their communities and nation. In Canada, where I come from, nationalism is expressed more quietly. For those youth, though, it was an important way of asserting who they were and their hopes for the future.

In Israel, I met adolescents who spoke of peace and ignored the danger that threatened them every day on the buses or in their cars or while playing on the beaches. Bombings, acts of terror and war, were so close, and yet youth simply moved on with their lives, making friends, dreaming about the future, being helpful to others.

In Colombia, a 10-year-old girl sold me a package of gum on the street, proud to be working and helping to support her family. In Pakistan, seven-year-olds work in lightbulb factories. In Turkey, pre-pubescent girls work willingly hooking silk rugs, preparing for the day they will be good enough to be employed as weavers entirely in their own right. I can sit here, snug in my North American home, and wish child labor was not a necessity for these children, but it is important that I see that the children themselves may experience their lives as successful.

In Sierra Leone and urban America, children take up arms to protect themselves. They are made to do unthinkably violent deeds to those they are convinced are their enemies by those who have much to gain by their hatred. By age 14 many of these children have known only war and violence and lived an adult's life for several years. When aid organizations or the police come and decommission child soldiers and neighborhood gangs, it is not surprising that these outsiders meet resistance. After all, what do we have to offer these children that they don't already have on their own terms: Power? Control? A sense of belonging? A meaningful role in their communities?

In the far north, among Aboriginal peoples, I met 11-year-olds who had gone truant from school to live on the land with their parents, forgoing the modern conveniences of television and central heating. These are children fiercely proud of their language and culture, even if they can barely read.

In a world of risk and contradiction, children weave unusual paths to health.

> ### CONVENTIONAL AND UNCONVENTIONAL WELL-BEING
>
> ➢ Children find the building blocks of health by taking advantage of whatever they have available.
> ➢ Different cultures define success differently.
> ➢ Teachers and caregivers engage youth best when efforts to promote health are tailored to the contexts in which they live.

Trouble and Truth

A team of researchers and I are trying to understand how children and youth the world over find health in chaotic situations like those I just described. What does it look like when children save themselves from living with despair? Even the middle-class child from a wealthy Western nation is sometimes vulnerable to this despair. Children feel the nameless commodification of being part of the machine we call *consumerism*. Pink Floyd's haunting refrain is as true now as it was two decades ago. We are all supposed to be "just another brick in the wall." Those who resist can find themselves in trouble—with teachers, parents, and communities who dismiss the young person's claim to truth as nothing but naive innocence that will cost them dearly.

We shouldn't dismiss what kids say so quickly.

There is a long list of characteristics that help youth survive the world over. Pandas, chameleons, and leopards all tell me that some combination of these personal, interpersonal, community, and cultural factors are what get them through life. However, none of these characteristics have only one way of being expressed. All three strategies to secure a powerful identity work to some extent in securing access to what youth need to be healthy.

For example, we tell adolescents, "Stay in school." But what does school look like? How many hours? Is it the full-time routine many teenagers experience in North America or the novel approaches used with child laborers in India, where children attend classes half days, while the rest of the time they make a "contribution" to their families and communities? Getting an education and making a contribution to one's community, both qualities associated with healthy youth, can be expressed in many different ways.

Similarly, and most sadly, youth show me that feelings of control can come just as easily from robbing someone as from saying no to drugs and alcohol.

Close and supportive relationships can be found among gang members and in sexual relationships as easily as with teachers, parents, and other caregivers.

Political participation is for some getting voted onto student council or being a writer for a community newspaper. For others, it can be achieved by joining a paramilitary outfit in South America, or closer to home, becoming a member of an Aboriginal warrior society that forces Western governments to honor treaty rights with First Nations peoples.

Some Choices Are Better Than Others

That's right. Some choices *are* better than others. Even the most adamant and armed individuals or those who work as child laborers insist that they would rather live in a world where they didn't need to express themselves in the ways that they do. We are, however, a long way from such an ideal world. The world we inhabit frequently leaves us few choices for powerful identities.

Derrick Jensen (2002) describes our illusion of choice as *The Culture of Make Believe* that glosses over the real issues confronting us: hatred, exploitation, the way we treat each other and our environment. His book is a tough read because it forces us to go beyond our hatred of those who do evil things to understanding how they do what they do in the name of power. He talks about the blind disregard people have for one another when they are doing what they are "supposed" to be doing according to the rules. He makes a convincing argument that while we are horrified by the actions of slave traders, CEOs of tobacco corporations, and those who torture animals to make cosmetics, we miss the point if we think that individuals themselves are always trying to be bad. They, like everyone else, are looking for something powerful to say about themselves.

Jensen (2002) wrestles with this, showing us his evolving thinking. Wondering aloud, he asks, "It's not about hate, is it?" No, he answers, it's not. "It's all about power" (pp. 82–82).

6

A New Way to Look at Bullying

It may be time to ask what views of social competence children themselves take, as this is likely to be of more practical use in intervention. . . . Bullying may be considered more socially competent [to children] than "being a weakling."

—Jon Sutton

Pandas, chameleons, and leopards live together on our playgrounds and inside our schools. Together they form an interesting weave of relationships: some good, some bad, some simply confusing to outsiders like us adults. No matter how troubling a student's behavior, though, it is important to understand that behavior as a way the youth nurtures resilience. There are many issues we could examine that present us with complex challenges: violence, drugs, dress, even the lack of civility in our schools. In this chapter, I'll look at just one of these: bullying. By looking closely at what bullying and being bullied mean to pandas, chameleons, and leopards, I will explore a template for how to understand this issue and many others as well. In particular, a look at what we think about bullies and bullying behaviors is a good way to critically assess and better understand the health-seeking strategies of our most vulnerable and troubling youth.

All is not quite as it seems on the playground.

We already know, for example, that the disruptive behavior of bullies takes place in the context of environments that make the bullying possible. We know we must change the environment in which youth live to one that is better monitored if we are to take away the opportunities for bullies to be powerful (Olweus, 1993). However, the pandalike bully doesn't get deterred so easily. It is just as important to help bullies cope in nonbullying ways by providing them with *alternatives* to violence that meet their needs and give them just as powerful a way of scripting their lives as successful.

Bullying as Coping: Jake

A dialogue I had with Jake, a 13-year-old boy who had had many suspensions in the past year for aggressive behavior at school, illustrates much of what I have found useful in my work with adolescents who bully. The flow of the conversation to follow reflects the six strategies discussed in previous chapters.

To understand Jake, one first has to understand his mother, Pamela. She has a remarkable story to tell. A street child by the age of 15, she was heavily addicted to drugs and repeatedly subjected to sexual abuse by a gang of boys in her community—all this before she ran away from home. In the years that followed, she had several children, of which only one still remains with her: Jake. Pamela's life is a history of despair except for her dedication to her son. She doesn't want him to repeat her mistakes and has made a point to reach out for help.

Still, the problems facing Pamela and Jake are large. The family has moved many times, avoiding problems with the police or Pamela's violent boyfriends or in search of a way to resolve Pamela's chronic unemployment. Each move brings with it another school and another set of friends for Jake. To make matters worse, Jake was sexually abused for three years when he was a preschooler by a neighbor who was subsequently jailed for his abuse of a number of small boys. Jake has responded to all this by becoming a fighter at school, allowing no one to pick on him or by keeping to himself; his computer games are sometimes his best playmates.

The story I just told is not, however, the full story about this family or about Jake. Through conversations with Pamela and Jake, I have come to see a hidden resilience disguised as dangerous, delinquent, deviant, even disordered behavior a child like Jake must use to survive and thrive.

Though there were lots of things we could have talked about, Jake and Pamela agreed that we'd start by trying to help Jake get along better at school and stop his aggressive behavior with other children. He'd already failed one grade because of it. He didn't want to fail another.

The following is a transcript of a conversation between the three of us during our second meeting together. Jake had been doing better since moving to his new school. He's had no suspensions in the six weeks he's been there, compared with four suspensions in the three months prior to the move. However, both Pamela and Jake are concerned that the pattern of aggression and suspensions will resume.

Michael (M):   Maybe you can help me understand, Pamela. When you made the last move, what was the motivation for that?

Pamela (P):   Moving back here? To get Jake on the right track. I've been involved in a lot of bad relationships, bad choices, when he was little. We lived in various places. Over the years he's been in 10 or 12 different places. Sometimes he's been back to the same school. Lots of times not. My mom and dad are really supportive. They'll let Jake go and stay with them when I need to get my feet under me.

M: *[Looking at both Jake and Pamela]* You've stayed connected to them? Your parents. Through all those moves?

P: They've been his rock. I usually end up back at Mom's when I really need a place to stay.

As with many of my conversations, I want to use this one to understand Jake's life in context. Just because Pamela experienced conflict in the past with her parents doesn't mean that those same parents, now grandparents, won't be a rock-solid support to Jake. Hearing a parent's truth, like hearing a youth's, means being open to hearing the unexpected.

M: So now that you're back, Jake, what's different?

Jake (J):   At my other school they just criticized or wouldn't help. If you did something wrong, if you couldn't understand or do something, they'd give you a lecture, a 20-minute lecture.

P: They never really helped him. He's never been very good at getting his thoughts down on paper.

M: Is this frustrating for you, Jake?

J: No. I just gave up after a while.

M: Just gave up?

J: Yeah, just gave up. I didn't want to do it anymore. I can be like that. Like if I can't get my lock to work on my locker, I'll just walk away.

M: Hmm, so there's this pattern of shutting things away, of walking away, of even moving away from problems, of coming back to your grandparents, your mom's parents. There's quite a story of dealing with things by shutting them away. Am I understanding this right?

P: It may not be the proper way, but it's the only way we both know what to do.

M: I don't know if it's proper or not. I don't necessarily have an opinion on that. But it does seem to be what has kept you going. That's interesting.

It would have been easy to have seen Jake's pattern of shutting things away as a sign of disorder. Far better, I reasoned, to understand this as his best choice of coping, given what resources he has (Strategy 1 reminds me to hear Jake's truth). By avoiding labeling the behavior as bad (or good), I avoid the resistance many people have experienced who have tried to help Pamela and Jake in the past. Of course, I know very little about what makes this pattern work. My role was next to help them both look critically at what Jake does and whether it works to his advantage (Strategy 2). I also became curious if there were any other coping strategies Jake uses.

P: That's not all of it. Sometimes Jake can be a real terror, too. He was like that when he was younger. He'd even haul off and belt me when he was even just a little kid.

M: What changed?

J: I just shut myself in my room rather than fighting.

P: It got to the point where my ex-husband Curtis couldn't control him when he was eight. And Curtis was this big man, who weighed like 365 lbs. It blew Curtis away that a little kid could be so strong. And Curtis was just so surprised—even when he just pushed him away and Jake hit the floor, he'd just get back up and attack again.

M: So things have changed.

P: I don't know what changed. He was on Ritalin for his ADHD. Now he's on Dexedrine. He was on too much of the Ritalin—seeing bugs in his cereal. Now just on school days, he takes 10 milligrams. Calms him right down. But I know he has it in him to be pretty wild. I know he'll defend himself. If a kid is picking on Jake at school, he'll defend himself.

J: I don't have to fight here. It's a better school. The teachers.

I'm beginning to see a pattern here. Jake's bullying behavior is both a point of pride for him (think how strong he must have felt as a little boy!) and a way of protecting himself. Even his mother, the most important member of his audience, applauds his capacity to defend himself when attacked. As Jake and Pamela tell me their story, I see very clearly that when provided opportunities where Jake feels safe, he will adapt easily and stop his bullying. In the process, I honor his version of the truth about surviving and thriving (Strategy 1). I also come to understand that he is open to change, but I suspect he'll only change in an environment where he feels he has something else important to say about himself, opportunities for a new way of seeing himself (Strategy 3). I wonder whether he has another, different identity to show us out among his friends in his new community.

M: There's less lecturing?

J: Yeah, and in the other school, you couldn't even make jokes. If you did, you were sent to the office.

M: Do you like making jokes?

J: No.

M: Do you like laughing at other people's jokes?

J: Yeah.

M: Do you have many friends?

J: No.

M: Will that change?

J: Yeah.

M: You said once before that you are pretty good at making new friends. Am I right about that? Do you have experience making friends?

J: Sort of.

M: I can't imagine making those all moves—between schools, friends, houses. I wouldn't be near as much an expert as you on how to do that.

J: Well, I just let friends come to me.

M: What do the other kids see when they look at you?

J: They think I'm tall. And sometimes weak, but not once they try to pick on me. Then I fight back, and that shows them I'm not weak.

M: What else happens when you push back?

J: I get suspended—for punching people in the head. But they stop. I get suspended for a couple of days, but they don't pick on me again.

M: Are you ever the one doing the picking?

J: No.

M: Do you find that other kids get picked on?

J: Yeah.

M: What do you do then? Do you ever defend them?

J: No. But like in Bridgewater, there were lots of people getting picked on. There were the town people and the shore people who got bused. I was a townie.

M: Did people look to you as a good fighter, fighter for the town?

J: Yeah. I don't back down.

In the foregoing conversation, I explore many different aspects of Jake's coping. My questions are aimed at understanding how his behavior changes and how others see him and to look critically (Strategy 2) at what he believes keeps him safe and feeling good about himself. To accomplish this, I ask him about other aspects of his bullying. Does he ever defend other children who are feeling the way he does? He doesn't, he says. Rather than condemning him or lecturing him about what is right and wrong, my questions explore the world as he understands it and the way he influences how others treat him. My words try to convey to him that I am sincerely curious why this pattern works for him so well. I don't applaud what he does, but I am getting to understand it better. My questions, employed in ways he can hear me (Strategy 4), help sustain our conversation. If I better understand what he does, I reason, I will be that much closer to finding a substitute that works both for Jake and those he hurts.

M: Hmm, that's interesting, you don't back down, and you don't let people pick on you.

J: No.

M: Like with your teachers. Even with adults. Or your stepdad, the story about you and Curtis.

J: Yeah.

M   So you have quite a long story about fighting back.

J: Yeah.

M: That's a very interesting story. Because on the one hand you have this story of shutting things away, like when you feel strong emotions or the lock on your locker won't work. You just walk away from problems. While in other parts of your life, you fight back. But sometimes the fighting back gets you into trouble, suspended.

J: Yes.

Jake has two different coping strategies. Both work well, at least from Jake's point of view. By offering them back to him, I am trying to find out whether what I see is actually how Jake experiences his world. I am telling him again, "I hear your truth." He agrees with me, which tells me that I now have something to work with. After all, Jake is not just another bully. He is a unique adolescent struggling to be different from everyone else. It's this search for differentness, Strategy 5, that is important to the progress of our work together.

M: Are there any good things to fighting back? Does anyone ever applaud you?

J: Yeah . . . me!

M: You? So you give yourself encouragement, to go for it.

J: Yeah, like in fifth grade, I got in trouble with my principal, and I had to sit in her music class, and then she was picking on me in front of these Grade 2s, and I yelled at her, and that got me suspended. I was suspended four times before Christmas.

M: In my books that would be a lot, but for you, I don't hear you saying that that was a problem.

J: Not for me.

M: Are there good things, then, about fighting back?

J: Yeah, then people don't pick on me. Getting suspended helps me. 'Cause then kids know I'll fight back.

M: But for your mom, it's a problem?

J: Yeah.

M: That's interesting because it seems that at school you use the fight-back kind of approach, and then in your personal life, you use the shut-yourself-off, draw-back approach. Are you happy with that difference?

J: Yeah.

M: Are you understanding at all why your mom is concerned about you using the attack, fight-back strategy at school?

J: Nope.

Often, conversations with teens like Jake deteriorate into one-word answers. It shouldn't be surprising that when I ask Jake if he understands his mother's concern, he answers "Nope," though when I summarized what looked like two coping strategies, he was much more willing to engage with me. My question about his mother was, after all, irrelevant. From Jake's point of view, it's more important that we adults understand why his behavior works for him. I strongly suspect this articulate young man knows his mother's concerns and has heard them many times. My question, posed from my vantage point as an adult, deserved the rebuke it got. I changed direction.

M: It's been interesting hearing about these two patterns. But if there was a way of you being in school and fighting back and not getting suspended, would you be interested in hearing about that?

J: Not really.

M: Not really? Can you help me understand that? In my world, suspensions are usually thought of as bad thing.

J: Well, I think it shows that when you get suspended for fighting back, it shows that you can't be picked on.

M: Oh, that makes sense. Let me write that down. [Taking notes] "If I'm suspended for fighting back, then I don't get picked on." So the only consequence, then, is that your mom worries?

J: And I get grounded.

M: Okay, so the only two bad things are that you get grounded and Mom worries. But there are also lots of good things. If I were to flip this around and talked about shutting things away at home, does that have any bad consequences?

J: None that I know.

Jake's Truth

In the foregoing dialogue, Jake tells me that what bullying means to him is something very different from what it means to me. For this panda, sticking to this pattern of aggression has helped him navigate his way through the turbulent waters of many, many disruptions in his life. But Jake isn't a panda with just one diet. He has *two* patterns of behavior that he uses to cope. He also ignores problems, walking away from feeling strong emotions. Though it might be easy to read "depression" and "conduct disorder" or even "dissociation" into Jake's behavior, all these diagnoses would overlook how adaptive his solutions have been.

By working with Jake and his mother to look at the good and bad things about both strategies, exploring opportunities with Jake for change, and making sure my words didn't dump on Jake what I think is the right way to handle his life, I got Jake remarkably interested in our conversation. Even better, he was able to show me how different he is from his peers. How unbullylike he sees himself. He doesn't tell jokes. He stands up for himself. He's not a weakling. He's loyal to others. Not a bad choice of identity, is it?

Jake's Substitutions

Of course, finding a substitute that would work, that would stop Jake from repeating the pattern of suspensions for violence that caused his mother so many worries in their last community, was a little more challenging. But Jake, by telling me about his life in such detail, gave me the clues I needed to find that substitute.

Here are four things my conversation with Jake helped me to learn about him:

- Jake wants to complete his school year and not be held back again, which means *he is committed to learning.*
- Jake wants other boys to see him as someone who is strong and won't put up with teasing, which means *he might be open to participating in organized sports, weight training or martial arts*—all of which teach discipline as they build physical capacity.
- Jake knows how to walk away from problems but tends to use that strategy only to cope with his emotions or to avoid thinking himself stupid and forgetful. Jake *might consider using his "walk-away" strategy when confronted with people who threaten him.*
- Jake *prides himself on being persistent and achieving goals* if they are important to him, even if the goal is only to show others he can defend himself and never back down.

Jake's Adaptations

Knowing all this about Jake, we helped him make decisions that showed his teachers and his mother that he could persist at his studies and pass his year without getting any more suspensions. Jake began to use the walk-away approach when he felt threatened and the attack-back approach when his emotions were hurt. It's been a good start, one that Pamela has been applauding. As Jake's best audience, her love and commitment has helped encourage Jake to keep making these changes. Now, when Jake is feeling that he has to prove something to other kids, he instead seeks the praise of the many adults and some old friends in his life who tell him what he needs to hear: "Better to walk away and pass the year. Leave the losers behind!"

With his mother, it's a bit different. Through the calm formality of the counseling session, Jake has begun to use his voice to "attack back" in a socially acceptable way. He began to tell his mother about his life, in particular about his abuse and what it has meant to him. It was easier for Jake to speak once Pamela opened up and shared her own struggles with her son.

Bullying and the Three Identities

Pandas as Bullies

It's not long since we thought about bullying as nothing more than the kind of behavior children did when in groups. It was abusive, and we knew to stop it when we saw it, but the *bullying industry* has created bullying as a social problem. On one level, this is a good thing. It has meant that many children don't have to put up with the shame of being a victim. But for children *who are looking* for a script to follow, it has also created another easily accessible way of being bad and powerful all at the same time

Perhaps this is why programs that seek to prevent bullying in schools sometimes have the unintended consequence of actually creating pro-bullying attitudes among youth. There are now several studies of short-term antibullying campaigns, like that of Leila Rahey and Wendy Craig (2002) in Canada and by Christina Salmivalli (2001) in Finland, showing that students who participate in these prevention programs wind up thinking that bullying is something they are *more likely* to do after learning what it is!

From the panda's point of view, this makes perfect sense. Inadvertently, some prevention programs offer students a powerful script that is theirs to act out. We adults come into their classrooms and tell them, "If you do this, you will get noticed." In fact, we describe everything they have to do in detail. What's more, we explain that bullies are often kids who are compensating for the abuse they've suffered or their own exclusion. We don't mean to, but we hand to vulnerable kids the perfect way of performing a new identity as something other than a victim.

The bully does what the bully does because it helps the bully survive. When we understand what the bully likes about being a bully, we are more likely to find other ways bullies can be bullylike in ways that are socially desirable.

Chameleons as Bystanders

Chameleons are more typically the bystanders or play slightly less passive roles as the bully's sidekicks. They are comfortable sharing the bully's power but are less committed to being bullies themselves. And why should they be? Their strength is being able to navigate between groups. They are comfortable resting in the bully's shadow. To do more would bring with it the negative aspects of being a bully: suspensions, angry parents, long conversations with school administrators, and referrals to counselors who would then think less of them.

Far better, the chameleons reason, to float, to borrow the bully's power once in a while, and then withdraw to safer places when the problems threaten to overwhelm the other, more positive identities the chameleons have fashioned themselves.

Leopards as Bullies and Defenders

Leopards are as likely to be reformed bullies as kids who have figured out how to stand up to bullies. Maybe it is their age, but now and then I meet older teens who have taken on the role as the protector of other children. These defenders may be gang leaders or children who have left delinquent peer groups after coming to the conclusion that they are fine just the way they are. In either case, they know they don't need to remain stuck in the singular role as the delinquent or the bully. They can say something more positive about themselves. One way they make this positive statement is by creating a shield around those more vulnerable than they are.

They are the ones who easily stand up for the teenager who is different or mentally or physically challenged. I'm surprised at how frequently it is the youth we would least likely expect to be defending others who are in fact the most passionate in that role.

What looks odd to us adults is one other way leopards extend their territory. Leopards say to the world that you have to negotiate with them how you are going to look at them and that you are also going to have to negotiate how you see other youth that are pushed aside and fall under a leopard's watchful eye.

This comes as no surprise to those who work with adolescents clinically, though it continues to baffle parents and school administrators. Jon Sutton and his colleagues caution us "to realize that some bullying children do have power, and that they can misuse this power in ways advantageous to them (in some circumstances). . . . They would probably not see their behavior as incompetent or maladaptive, and there is evidence that it often is not. However, their bullying behavior is socially undesirable" (Sutton, Smith, & Swettenham, 1999).

Therein lies the challenge. How can we see the bully as holding skills that can be used in any number of different ways? It is this perspective, however, that opens doors to helping youth like this move from being bullies who *harm* others to being bullies who *protect*. Even Dan Olweus (1993), the grandfather of bullying research, has found that self-esteem is frequently high in these young people. Our trick as their educators and caregivers is to offer them the chance to be their same selves in more positive ways.

BULLIES AND COPING

➤ Bullying occurs in context: Bullies use opportunities to bully as a survival strategy.

➤ Bullying behavior can successfully build bullies' images of themselves as powerful, respected, and in control.

➤ Bullies change when equally powerful opportunities for success are made available and are realistically attainable.

Providing Opportunities for Adaptation

The implications of understanding that youth are pandas, chameleons, and leopards—or for that matter, deer, wild dogs, and antelope and any other description of young people's identities that they endorse—is that our relationship with youth shifts in focus from control to one that opens possibilities for youth to adapt.

Too much effort is targeted toward *stopping* youth from behaving in one way or the other. Often, efforts that force youth to stay in school, remain celibate, say "No" to drugs, do as their parents tell them, and fit in where they should are ineffective at best and frequently harmful. They can corner youth into patterns of resistance with no way out but more and more self-destructive behavior. *I prefer instead to ask youth to do more of the things I see that I like them doing rather than asking them to do less of what they tell me keeps them feeling strong.*

Substitutions for Bullies

Take for example the interactions of bullies like Geoffrey, whom I introduced in the first chapter, and those they bully. We will be much more likely to change bullies when we appreciate what they do and why. When we affirm the small bit of good (and I realize this is a controversial thing to do) in how they cope, then we can offer them a less destructive alternative. But this alternative must help them do more of whatever it was that made them feel like somebody important when they played the dangerous, delinquent, deviant, or disordered teen.

In my experience, most bullies, if we are to call them that, describe themselves as pandas. To hear their descriptions of their behavior, there are as many good things about being a bully as there are bad. These are our youth's own complex stories that support a self-definition as resilient. When I take the time to really listen with an open mind, I hear about victimized children who learn to victimize others. I hear about teens with little sense of who they are or what they have to offer who find through their bullying behavior a clearly more powerful self-definition. I hear about lives lived in the neutered wastelands of secure suburbs where there are few risks, few rites of passage, and even less attention to an adolescent's need to impress others with grandiose displays. In those contexts, too, the actions of the bully can make sense to the teenager trying to be something other than the lame consumer mass marketers want our teens to be.

Oddly, we often forget that advantaged kids bully, too. They can intimidate through overt consumerism, keeping others in their place by adhering to the misguided notion that "I am what I can buy."

> Rich or poor, youth resist the pull of mediocrity. They seek the stimulation of excess. They don't want to simply fit in with expectations others place on them. When they are forced to do so, the result can be an angry teen who feels entitled to a special status. It is this entitlement that blinds the bully to the effect his or her behavior has on others.

The Many Faces of the Bully

My description of bullies draws me away from understanding them as simply victims, victimizers, or some combination of both. Instead, the bullies I meet implicate their families, schools, and communities in the unfortunate drama that has become their lives. Pandas, chameleons, and leopards are vigilant for opportunities to make themselves feel powerful.

The problem is one that schools alone are sorely inadequate to address. The powerful identities that bullies find at school are ones that they carry from one set of relationships to the next. We may be able to control the Geoffreys in our classrooms, but we don't change them unless they find other identities that are every bit as powerful as the ones we ask them to shed.

Fortunately, because youth are embedded in matrices of relationships, the vast warp of positive associations and weave of negative attention that is found in all communities offer youth endless possibilities to develop new ways of being themselves. If I have learned anything from these youth, it is to be optimistic.

Substitutions for Victims

Of course, the other piece of this puzzle is the victims, the children who are bullied. We have a responsibility to keep them safe, to create environments where they can flourish in ways other than as victims. I believe we are most effective when we help pandas, those youth stuck in their identities as worthless, to become better at navigating between peer groups. Bullied children are far less often targets for bullies when they are able to take on multiple identities. Playing the chameleon is their easiest salvation. They do better when they can say back to the bully, "No, you've got it wrong, I'm not your victim. I am _____, and I know it because that is how others see me." Beware, though, the children or adolescents who learn to resist the demeaning put-downs and derogatory self-definitions on the playground are likely to carry that talent into the classroom and back home.

Unfortunately, we don't often enter into conversations with kids stuck in states of victimhood about what their options really are. What if they became delinquent? What if they became powerful, like the bully? What if they resisted authority? I certainly don't want children to move from being victims to being delinquents, but I know many that do. It shouldn't surprise us. When I at least talk about these options, which the children are usually already considering, I am better able to identify what the bullied child is really seeking. I'm then in a better position, as I am with bullies, to offer the child something other than a problem identity.

We need to open opportunities for youth to learn how to resist the labels others stick to them. As painful as it can be, we must let youth shake the shackles of the labels we adults also wish upon them, giving youth the space to learn how to be critical consumers of all possible selfhoods.

Years after being bullied by Geoffrey in seventh grade, I now understand how shortsighted my teacher's advice had been. I was told, with the best of intentions, "OK, you're a bright kid, you can be you. Don't let Geoffrey get to you." The advice sadly missed the point. If I am honest with myself now, I know that I wanted what Geoffrey had, every bit as much as I believe Geoffrey wanted what I had. I didn't just want to be a smart kid, I wanted to have my identity as the smart kid recognized by kids like Geoffrey just as much as kids who behaved like me.

BULLIED CHILDREN

> ➢ The bullied child may long for the same power the bully has.
> ➢ The bullied child needs to be offered an identity other than "victim" that is vested with power.
> ➢ Bullied children become bullies when no other equally powerful identity is offered.

Escape Plans

There is something about us that drives us to resist conformity, to seek power. We understand, even as children, that we have to repeat our behavior over and over again if we are going to convince others we are who we want to be known as.

I didn't need to become a bully to escape my status as victim. I was one of the fortunate ones who had other ways to express myself. I left home at 16, I traveled, and I became independent and self-supporting. Along the way, I found a role for myself of being an outspoken advocate for kids like Geoffrey. It's been a great solution, one that lets me be Geoffreylike in socially acceptable ways.

7

Assessing
Resilience

If power were never anything but repressive, if it never did
anything but to say no, do you really think one would be brought
to obey it? What makes power hold good, what makes it accepted,
is simply the fact that it doesn't only weigh on us as a force that
says no; it also traverses and produces things, it induces pleasure.
—Michel Foucault

If we are going to offer pandas, chameleons, and leopards less
destructive, more prosocial alternatives that bring equally powerful
identities, we need an inventory of these young people's strengths.
Resilience is a cluster of resources: individual, relational, community,
and cultural. Resources for health, the factors that make it more likely
people experience themselves as healthy, are often in short supply for
youth who face multiple risks associated with violence, poverty,
addictions, mental illness, or just the bland overprotectiveness of a
society full of fear. Access to resources is the gift we give youth
through our interventions in our schools and communities.

In previous chapters, I discussed the principle of substitution,
offering youth new ways to sustain their resilience. Each of the six
associated strategies helps us to get it right when we offer youth substitutes for their problem identities. In this chapter, I present a way of
assessing adolescents' strengths. As teachers and counselors, we are
better able to offer teenagers powerful identity choices when we know

1. What strengths they already have that we can build on

2. What they lack and therefore need us to supplement in order for them to experience themselves as powerful, healthy, and resilient

3. How they use their strengths to maintain identities as resilient (though teenagers' expressions of their strengths may not always meet with our approval)

The Resilient Youth Strengths Inventory

The Resilient Youth Strengths Inventory (RYSI) is an easy-to-use tool that provides a flexible portrayal of young people's strengths. It can be tailored to each adolescent. As such, *it is not meant to label youth,* but instead, to offer an overview of the areas of strength found in a young person's life. Combined with the questions that follow the instrument, educators and caregivers will be able to see clearly what it is they need to offer to help the teen become more resilient in conventional ways. Strengths expressed in troubling ways will need more socially acceptable outlets. Strengths that are shown to be in short supply will need to be shored up with more and better resources.

An International Collaboration

A short while ago, I had the good fortune to bring people together from around the world to help explain why kids survive well, beating the odds given the risks they face. I heard from people from a Northern Aboriginal community; Eastern Canadians; researchers from Colombia, Hong Kong, and southern Florida; a priest from India; urban youth workers from the prairies; a psychologist from Moscow; a social activist from Tanzania; young peer educators from Gambia; the CEO of a human rights organization in Palestine; and university colleagues specializing in trauma and stress in Israel. They all shared their insights into what makes youth survive.

The diversity of their suggestions is likely to be matched only by the diversity we can find within our own communities. The more we talked, the more I saw that while there are many things we hold in common the world over, we share many differences, too. Those differences are also apparent in our own communities. We each have tended to frame the problem of youth survival in very narrow ways. "If only Sam would go back to school." "If only Kate would stop having sex with boys."

It's not that easy. Kate and Sam, the two youth I introduced in Chapter 5, both have their own stories to tell. No comprehensive list of factors that could save them from the risks they perceive could ever be complete until we talk with the youth themselves.

For three years, a team of researchers that I lead has been interviewing youth from across North America and around the world. We developed the Child and Youth Resilience Measure (CYRM; Ungar, Lee, Callaghan, & Boothroyd, in press), a 58-item self-report instrument that looks at individual, relational, community, and cultural aspects of resilience of relevance to people in many different cultures. Our results from the first phase of the research show that aspects of resilience have both universal and culture-specific aspects. If we are going to understand our youth, we have to balance what we think we know about *all* youth with an appreciation for our own youth's unique coping strategies and social ecologies.

The RYSI has been adapted from the CYRM. The questions have been modified to ask caregivers about the resilience of young people in their care. The Inventory is not meant to be used as a standardized psychometric test, with predictive qualities. Instead, it is a tool to help us as teachers, parents, and other caregivers to look critically at what we think we know about the young people with whom we interact. The RYSI has been used with hundreds of workshop participants and is now part of a larger multiyear study of resilience among youth worldwide.

Thirty-two Signs

As a multidisciplinary and international group, my colleagues and I agreed that there are at least 32 separate things we as educators and caregivers can begin to recognize that have an impact on teenager's resilience. These are some of the signposts we can look for if we want to know if youth are likely to do well.

Pandas find ways to experience these 32 things. The same is true for chameleons and leopards. Understanding what is working for our adolescents begins with understanding how they achieve each of these 32 health indicators. Before reviewing this list of items, it's important to remember the following:

- Don't get stuck thinking there is only one way to express each of these characteristics or to find these health-sustaining resources. After all, for some kids, playing the delinquent may be their ticket to food, medical care, an education, and attention. It would be nice if it weren't so, but understanding resilience begins with understanding how kids negotiate for their health status in the context in which they live.
- Feel free to add items to this list that are unique to the adolescent's culture and your own. Every community offers teenagers unique opportunities to be themselves while demanding certain behaviors that are the benchmarks of health.

- Think about how the adolescent sees his or her world. Are you sure that just because the teen is drifting into trouble, there is nothing good happening *from the teen's point of view?*
- Talk with others who know the youth. Our identities are not the result of what one person mirrors back to us. Think carefully who might have a different opinion than yours about the teen. Who might agree with you?

A Measure of Resilience

Thinking about a young person you teach, who is in your care or under your supervision (as in a school or other institution), read each of the statements on the RYSI that are presented on the following pages, and circle the number that best describes the extent to which that statement is true for the adolescent. There are, of course, no right or wrong answers. In fact, if a question on the Inventory doesn't apply to a student you are concerned about or you simply don't know (which could be a hint of something that you will need to discuss with the youth), you can simply not answer the question. Just answer those questions to which you have answers. I've presented the Inventory in four sections to make it easier to complete.

You will also find spaces at the end of each section for including your own questions about teenagers' resilience. It is important to remember that the Inventory is *just one possible grouping* of all the many factors that can contribute to adolescents' health in different contexts and cultures. There are likely personal characteristics of students of yours that you think help them grow up well. What do you think young people most need to overcome adversity and stress?

Feel free to include as many questions as you like under each section.

Individual Characteristics

The first 23 questions deal with aspects of the adolescent's personality. These questions explore 13 of the 32 different resilience-related factors:

- Assertiveness
- Problem solving
- Feelings of personal control
- Living with uncertainty
- Self-awareness
- Social support
- Optimism
- Empathy for others
- Goals and aspirations
- Independence and dependence
- Attitudes toward drugs and alcohol
- Sense of humor
- Sense of duty

The Resilient Youth Strengths Inventory—Individual

To what extent does each statement describe the youth?	Not at All	A Little	Some-what	Quite a Bit	A Lot
1. Is comfortable asking for help	1	2	3	4	5
2. Can solve own problems	1	2	3	4	5
3. Keeps going even when life gets difficult	1	2	3	4	5
4. Believes that own actions today will influence his or her future	1	2	3	4	5
5. Feels confident in challenging and confusing situations	1	2	3	4	5
6. Is aware of personal strengths	1	2	3	4	5
7. Is aware of personal weaknesses	1	2	3	4	5
8. Is comfortable with self-expression in close relationships with peers	1	2	3	4	5
9. Is comfortable with own sexual expression	1	2	3	4	5
10. Feels a part of a group when with friends	1	2	3	4	5
11. Knows that family, friends, and relatives will be supportive during difficult times	1	2	3	4	5
12. Thinks most problems in life will get solved in a positive way	1	2	3	4	5
13. Empathizes with others when bad things happen to them, even if he or she doesn't like them	1	2	3	4	5
14. Understands others' feelings	1	2	3	4	5
15. Has a vision of how the future should be	1	2	3	4	5
16. Strives to finish started projects	1	2	3	4	5

(Continued)

(Continued)

To what extent does each statement describe the youth?	Not at All	A Little	Some-what	Quite a Bit	A Lot
17. Cooperates with people around him or her	1	2	3	4	5
18. Can solve problems without using nonprescription drugs or alcohol	1	2	3	4	5
19. Uses fun and laughter to help solve problems in life	1	2	3	4	5
20. People think he or she is fun to be with	1	2	3	4	5
21. Thinks it is important to serve the community	1	2	3	4	5
22. Believes in personal responsibility to help make the world a better place	1	2	3	4	5
23. Has a sense of being at least as good as peers	1	2	3	4	5
(Add your own questions here)					
	1	2	3	4	5
	1	2	3	4	5

Relationships

The second set of seven questions asks about the adolescent's relationships with others at school and at home. These questions ask you to think about four different areas of a young person's life:

- The quality of caregiving the youth receives
- Competence in social situations
- Mentors
- Meaningful relationships

The Resilient Youth Strengths Inventory—Relationships

To what extent does each statement describe the youth?	Not at All	A Little	Some-what	Quite a Bit	A Lot
24. Caregivers watch the youth closely and know what the youth is up to when not at home.	1	2	3	4	5
25. Talks with family members about personal feelings	1	2	3	4	5
26. Is comfortable talking with new people	1	2	3	4	5
27. Knows how to behave in different social situations	1	2	3	4	5
28. Admires some adults	1	2	3	4	5
29. Feels supported by friends at school	1	2	3	4	5
30. Feels comfortable talking with teachers or other adults in the community about personal problems	1	2	3	4	5
(Add your own questions here)					
	1	2	3	4	5
	1	2	3	4	5

Community

The third set of 14 questions has to do with the adolescent's community and school and opportunities he or she has to be meaningfully involved in them. There are eight topics covered:

- Age-appropriate work
- Exposure to violence
- The government's role keeping kids safe and healthy
- Rites of passage
- Adult tolerance for the adolescent's behavior
- Safety and security
- Social equality
- Access to schooling

The Resilient Youth Strengths Inventory—Community

To what extent does each statement describe the youth?	Not at All	A Little	Some-what	Quite a Bit	A Lot
31. Has a job or volunteer work appropriate for his or her age	1	2	3	4	5
32. Has opportunities to develop job skills that will be useful later in life	1	2	3	4	5
33. Is able to avoid violent situations at home, at school, and in the community	1	2	3	4	5
34. Knows where to go to get help	1	2	3	4	5
35. Caregivers respect his or her sexual expression	1	2	3	4	5
36. Has opportunities to show evidence of becoming an adult	1	2	3	4	5
37. Is encouraged by family or community to seek nonviolent solutions to deal with people who break the law	1	2	3	4	5
38. Forgives family and community members who do unacceptable things	1	2	3	4	5
39. Eats enough most days	1	2	3	4	5
40. Feels safe with family members	1	2	3	4	5
41. Is treated fairly in the community	1	2	3	4	5
42. Feels it is important to get an education					
43. Teachers and other students make him or her feel a sense of belonging at school	1	2	3	4	5
(Add your own questions here)					
	1	2	3	4	5
	1	2	3	4	5
	1	2	3	4	5

Culture

Finally, we need to look much more broadly. Of all the types of questions that we could ask our adolescents about their resilience, these are the most unique and overlooked. It's not often that we stand back and think of our culture, nor are we very often asked to consider what other cultures can offer us when examining resilience. The world over, these are important questions to consider. They include seven resilience related factors, bringing the total number to 32:

- Religious affiliation
- Tolerance
- Shifting cultural values
- Social responsibility
- Life philosophy
- Cultural identification
- Cultural roots

The Resilient Youth Strengths Inventory—Culture

To what extent does each statement describe the youth?	Not at All	A Little	Some-what	Quite a Bit	A Lot
44. Participates in organized religious activities	1	2	3	4	5
45. Finds strength in religious or spiritual beliefs	1	2	3	4	5
46. Openly disagrees with caregivers and elders when their opinions differ	1	2	3	4	5
47. His or her family values are similar to those of the community	1	2	3	4	5
48. Adults in the community tolerate the ideas and strong beliefs of the youth	1	2	3	4	5
49. The community culture teaches ways to become a better person	1	2	3	4	5
50. Believes life should be lived in a certain way	1	2	3	4	5

(Continued)

(Continued)

To what extent does each statement describe the youth?	Not at All	A Little	Some-what	Quite a Bit	A Lot
51. Enjoys family and community traditions	1	2	3	4	5
52. Is proud to be (fill in nationality)	1	2	3	4	5
53. Is proud to be (fill in ethnic background)	1	2	3	4	5
54. His or her family has a routine around mealtimes	1	2	3	4	5
55. Knows where parents and grandparents were born	1	2	3	4	5
(Add your own questions here)					
	1	2	3	4	5
	1	2	3	4	5

So What Does It All Mean?

Most people who fill out the RYSI find that it forces them to look more closely at a youth and to consider areas of the young person's life that bolster well-being. Please add up the number of ones, the number of twos, and so on that you circled on the Inventory. Then tally the scores in *each column*. Finally, tally the combined column scores. I've included a blank form to show how this is done.

The final total gives a very simple approximation of a youth's strengths. It is important to remember that the factors that contribute to an adolescent's resilience combine exponentially. By this I mean that they don't just add up one on top of the other. *The more there are, the greater and greater their effect.* A youth who has just a few strengths makes it through life reasonably well. Those few strengths, factors associated with resilience, combine to balance out all of the adolescent's weaknesses. Having one characteristic that bolsters resilience is good. Two is even better, of course. But the real bump up in life comes when we start having three, which is really experienced as if we had four. If good fortune comes our way and we have four characteristics or resources that help make us resilient, it is the equivalent of eight good things to say about ourselves. And on it goes!

Youth's Name: _____

Answer Column	Number of times you choose this answer	Multiplied by:	The Column Number	Equals:	Total score for each column and overall total
Ones		x	1	=	
Twos		x	2	=	
Threes		x	3	=	
Fours		x	4	=	
Fives		x	5	=	
Total Score					

ASSESSING RESILIENCE

➢ Resilience factors combine exponentially, meaning the impact of each in combination is greater than each individually.
➢ Pandas, chameleons, and leopards can all score well on factors related to resilience, though they achieve resilience differently.

Evaluating Fairly

The most difficult part of completing the RYSI will be avoiding the blinders that most of us adults wear when we try to evaluate young people's lives. I suspect our own teachers and caregivers suffered from the same uneasiness with our lifestyle choices, our friends, and the paths we traveled toward health.

Take a school where the expectation by teachers is that all students must learn to play an instrument or participate in an equivalent extracurricular activity, for example. Certainly, music is one of those gifts we give children that last them a lifetime. There is, of course, nothing wrong with wanting children to develop musical ability.

Too often, however, best intentions turn into pitched battles. Some students resist vehemently. Others just drive their teachers and parents crazy with their choices of instrument or the music they want to learn to play. After all, are we willing to accept a rock band as equivalent to a school band? Are we willing to see music played on a synthesizer as being just as valuable as the music played by a teenager who excels at classical music on a more traditional instrument?

Scoring the Difficult Teen

How do we score, then, a teenager like Paula who has agreed to take up an instrument but who has shaved her head and begun to play in a metal-inspired, world beat band with three other girls she met while playing in her school band in junior high? Clearly, she is aware of her own strengths (after all, she's using her musical talent). That scores her high on Question 6. Her teachers and caregivers know what she is up to outside her home (if they are lucky enough to know the other band members and the place they rehearse). That scores her high on number 24. She is definitely showing that she can take on responsibility, and, if the band gets a gig or two, these are wonderful rites of passage through which teenagers show the world what they can do. I'd score her a four or five on number 36 as well. It's also a safe bet she is openly disagreeing with what her elders believe, maybe even her teachers, so let's give her another high score on number 46.

> The resilient adolescent is likely to show some strengths in all aspects of his or her life. For youth with less resilience, our role as caregivers is to look at our adolescents realistically and offer opportunities for them to find the health-sustaining resources they need. Only youth can tell us for sure what resources fit best for them.

Of course Paula might not be doing well in other parts of her life. Her defiant lifestyle might be making her less tolerant of others and unresponsive to how they feel. I'd score her low on number 14. She may not feel comfortable speaking with any adults, teachers included, having written them all off as out of touch with her world. This brings her down on Question 30. Likewise, often, the rock star personality comes with near starvation, the emaciated look of young women rockers. I might give her a two or a three on number 39. Finally, she may feel that because of her shaved head or because she is a girl, she's not being treated very fairly by others. Score her low on number 41.

You may notice that the fact Paula is upsetting her teachers and parents and is getting a reputation as a defiant, nasty kid in her school does not necessarily mean that what she is doing doesn't work well for her. It can be difficult for her teachers to look at what they perceive as antisocial behavior in a prosocial light. When filling out the RYSI, be careful that you are not judging an adolescent's coping strategies more harshly than they need to be judged. On the other hand, be fair and call it as you see it. Just because youth are acting badly doesn't mean that some things in their lives aren't working well. But this is very personal; our young rock star might be coping fine, but another band member may be far less resilient and at much greater risk.

8

Translating the Results of the Resilient Youth Strengths Inventory

"When did trouble at school first come along?"

"Trouble" had been around Alan since the third grade…

"Well, who won out this week when you tally up the results? How many wins for you, Alan, and how many wins for Trouble?" asked Ron.

Alan hadn't quite thought about it in those terms. "Well, I guess Trouble won," said Alan, feeling defeated.

—John Winslade & Gerald Monk

Though it is not always the case, I most often encounter pandalike students whose teachers would score them lower on the Resilient Youth Strengths Inventory (RYSI) discussed in the last chapter just as the students themselves have come to expect. Because these teens are either typically denied opportunities or overlook and avoid opportunities when they come about, pandas tend to have low scores when their caregivers complete the Inventory.

Pandas Shoot

If one remembers, pandas like to do the same thing over and over again. These are youth who have a few strengths that serve them very well, but they are also likely to have patterns of behavior, or lack access to opportunities, that put them at much more risk than other youth. They keep shooting for gold but only score when conditions are just right.

As educators concerned with the development (and survival) of these students, we need to look hard for good things to say about these youth. For example,

Question 2: Can solve own problems when needed

> Pandas are often very good at solving problems, only they use one strategy (violence? running away?) over and over again.

Question 28: Admires some adults

> While we would likely score most kids who get into trouble with the law or are truant from school low on most of the relationship questions, they often score high on having adults whom they admire (adult criminals? sports stars? television video jockeys?).

Question 40: Feels safe with family members

> What about the street kid and the kid's street family? I meet many youth whom I score high on this item because they have found a group of other adolescents to be with that makes them feel safe. The fact that they are stuck in the life of the street child doesn't take away from the good things that street families offer to runaways and throwaways.

Question 46: Openly disagrees with caregivers and elders when their opinions differ

> You've got to hand it to pandas; they are seldom subtle in their disagreements. They express their disregard frequently and loudly, though seldom in ways that are socially acceptable.

Chameleons Score

In contrast, chameleons score higher more often on these items. They don't keep doing the same thing over and over again. These are youth who can flex. They go out looking for the resources and experiences they need to be healthy, although inside they may still be far less secure, hesitant to assert to the world, "This is who I am!" Their teachers tend to see more strengths.

Question 14: Understands others' feelings

> Chameleons excel at reading how other people are feeling. It is why they are so successful in navigating between peer groups. They are constantly in tune with what others need, trying to please them in order to fit in.

Question 26: Is comfortable talking with new people

> The chameleon needs to keep meeting new people to try to find a powerful identity. These kids are often great at making friends because they adapt to whatever people want them to be.

Question 33: Is able to avoid violent situations at home, at school, and in the community

> Because chameleons can navigate between groups, they seldom have to remain anywhere that feels threatening. If the street becomes too dangerous, they are just as likely to go back to school. Their goal is to find a powerful identity, not put themselves in harm's way.

Question 45: Finds strength in religious or spiritual beliefs

> Chameleons will often talk about their beliefs. Don't be surprised if they change, however, as chameleons experiment with new religions and new beliefs.

Leopards Win

Leopards might laugh at the very thought of caregivers being asked to evaluate their lives. How dare anyone, least of all an adult, cast judgment on the life of a kid?! In some ways, I'd agree. This entire exercise of making sense of our children's lives is *for us adults.* It is *our* perceptions of the youth. Leopards resist others' labeling of them. They want to convince us they are doing just fine. I find that most teachers with leopards for students are happy to be convinced a youth is a leopard when the youth is doing what is expected. Leopards, however, can be overlooked when teachers and other caregivers find it hard to see all the good things happening in the young person's life.

Question 9: Is comfortable with own sexual expression

> The leopard's teachers, parents, clergy, and school nurses may worry, but leopards are usually adolescents who decide for themselves if they are going to be sexually active or not. For them, sex is a form of self-expression like everything else in their lives.

Question 24: Caregivers watch the youth closely and know what the youth is up to when outside the home

> Leopards are not shy about bringing their street personalities to school or back home, so teachers, parents, and other caregivers usually have a good idea who the adolescent's friends are. Leopards like the security of having someone looking out for them, someone who is taking notice of their lives, even if they won't do what they are told.

Question 43: Teachers and other students give him or her a sense of belonging at school.

> Leopards can't be leopards without environments that offer them the opportunities to be healthy. Fortunately, many teenagers who learn to assert a positive identity have learned how to do this in schools where teachers and administrators have made them feel welcome no matter how they want to present themselves to others.

Question 52: Is proud to be (fill in nationality)

> It shouldn't surprise us that leopards are proud of all aspects of who they are. Only don't count on them agreeing with the adults in their lives on what it means to be one nationality or another. Leopards are likely to try to redefine what it means to be a citizen in ways that can rankle their elders.

SEEKING RESILIENCE

➤ Children's behavior, good or bad, is a search for health.

➤ Resilience is a child's capacity to overcome adversity and access the resources necessary to succeed.

➤ A child's definition of health is something negotiated between the child and the child's teachers and caregivers

---

Shirley: A more resilient youth

People are drawn to Shirley the moment they meet her. She's 15, dresses in cast-off clothes from the thrift store, likes to leave her hair long and lets it fall across her face. Meeting her, you might think her odd, but then again, you wouldn't necessarily guess all the challenges Shirley has had to overcome at home. After getting to know her, you'd have to wonder if it hasn't been these hardships that have made her stand out from her peers. Everyone likes this vivacious young woman, at least everyone except her homeroom teacher.

Shirley is one of those free-thinking, in-your-face type of kids who never stop challenging. At home she acts like another parent. She has to have a say over how everything is done. She sees it as her role to make sure everyone knows she is just as competent as they are. She likely is, most days. An older brother, Paul, has been in and out of the hospital for the past two years with depression. Shirley has been the one he relies on most. She's played the confidante, helping to advocate for him when people don't do what's in his best interest. It's a role she likes.

Her mother, Carolyn, has also begun to rely on her for the help she provides. Her father, David, acts differently. He wants to look after his son his own way and resents Shirley for being so quick to tell him what Paul needs. Shirley figures her father is embarrassed by his son and wants to deny that he needs the medications, the attention of the psychiatrists, and the family therapy. David's anger at his daughter is safer for him than anger at his son. Shirley avoids what fights she can, but she doesn't back down entirely. She visits Paul, listens to her mom when she cries, and gets sad and even stands there and takes it from her dad.

It's Shirley's mother who can see what her daughter is all about. She laughs when she's called to the school and told that Shirley is going to be suspended again if she doesn't hold her tongue, doesn't complete all her assignments on time, or doesn't dress the right way for gym class. Shirley just never figured out that she was supposed to be a kid and do what kids are told to do. She's much more comfortable as the parent, even if she lives in a kid's body.

It was a welcome relief for Carolyn and Shirley's teacher, Pam, to be asked to fill out the Resilient Youth Strengths Inventory together during a consultation with me. I asked them to seek agreement on each item. Though it took a while, their final scores clearly offered them both hope. Shirley's brother's illness wasn't necessarily destroying Shirley's family. It had made things tough, but thankfully, Shirley was as resilient as both her mother and teacher had always suspected. Completing the instrument, they could see the sources of that strength more clearly. The following score sheet shows their totals.

Youth's Name: **Shirley**

Answer Column	Number of times you choose this answer	Multiplied by:	The Column Number	Equals:	Total score for each column and overall total
Ones	2	x	1	=	2
Twos	0	x	2	=	0
Threes	5	x	3	=	15
Fours	17	x	4	=	68
Fives	32	x	5	=	160
Total Score					245

Cam: A less resilient youth

Cam's got brains and a fair bit of athletic talent. His marks at school are passable. He has never been in trouble with the law, though since he is only 13, his principal would likely just say cynically, "He's got time yet."

Cam is also biracial. His mother, a dancer, is black. His father is white and a corporal in the military. They have a nice home in the suburbs. Most of their neighbors are white. That's fine for Cam. He and his older brother, Will, are popular with the girls in his neighborhood. They look more black than white and dress in baggy clothes. They don't get into any more or less trouble than any other kids. But you can see when you meet them that both boys are feeling the exclusion. They are feeling lost. They're not really sure how to live where they live. So they fall back to images they see in the media.

Cam's mother doesn't like it when her son takes on a street-smart look. "He's not street smart," she says. "He's a middle-class kid growing up in the 'burbs." End of story.

But that's not Cam's story. His story is about being given one detention after another for the past two years—for being late coming back from the bathroom, for wearing a bandana. He rolls his eyes. He uses the F word with his friends. He won't pull his pants up.

It's making Cam more and more angry. Whereas his older brother avoids the problems, Cam's taking it all personally. And why shouldn't he? He observes daily that black students are treated very differently from their white counterparts. Cam doesn't take prejudicial treatment in stride. He has begun instead to drift into patterns of hanging around with youth he doesn't even really like but who accept him as a powerful young black kid. His marks are slipping. He doesn't feel very good about himself. His mother and father are worried. They have good reason to be.

Cam should be more resilient; at least, you might expect it when you meet him. But the treatment he's received in school has beaten him down. In fact, black students are often much more likely to receive suspensions than whites (Cross, 2003). Hanging out with a less than desirable crowd wasn't always Cam's first choice for a coping strategy. He tried to play sports but kept being asked to leave teams when he missed practices because of suspensions. Schools, of course, want to avoid speaking about racism. When parents of youth like Cam come in to speak with school staff and administrators, school personnel are polite, but they're not taking any responsibility for what's happening, either.

Even filling in the Inventory, we couldn't find a lot to be optimistic about. But we did find a road map that will help us know what to offer Cam. After completing the questions, it was clear that community and cultural factors are the biggest burdens in Cam's life. The challenge is that these issues need more than clinical work. Stephen Madigan (1998), a family therapist who has worked with youth like Cam, talks about the need for a community to stand up to racism. Professionals who work with youth trapped by racism need to offer them a way to describe their experience that separates them from the problems they face. The racism that Cam experiences is something all of us need to confront if it's to change.

Here's how Cam scored when his mother filled out the Inventory. There are a few good things to say, but the results mostly tell us that Cam is a kid more at risk than one might have first thought, looking from the outside in. For the sake of comparison, it's useful to remember that Shirley scored 245.

Youth's Name: **Cam**

Answer Column	Number of times you choose this answer	Multiplied by:	The Column Number	Equals:	Total score for each column and overall total
Ones	13	x	1	=	13
Twos	23	x	2	=	46
Threes	16	x	3	=	48
Fours	3	x	4	=	12
Fives	1	x	5	=	5
Total Score					124

Using Results to Inform Our Efforts

The quick look at youths made possible by the RYSI offers many different signposts to watch for as the youth grows. It can help us as educators identify places to offer youth help. If you found yourself scoring a young person high in one area, like personal control, or another, like a strong ethnic identity, but thought that he or she was expressing this part of life in dangerous or destructive ways, that is helpful information to have. Pandas, chameleons, and leopards will change when someone appreciates the brilliance of how they already cope before offering them a powerful alternative.

> The more youth experience themselves as resilient and are provided the opportunities to feel that way, the better they are able to cope with adversity and stress and the better able they are as well to convince others they are healthy.

So Is Bad "Good"? Or Is It Still Bad?

How you score a young person on the Inventory gives insight into the question, "Is the adolescent healthy even if he or she is up to no good?" Pandas, chameleons, and leopards make the best possible use of the resources they have to sustain resilience. As teachers and caregivers, counselors and concerned citizens, we can offer adolescents who are experiencing resilience through dangerous, delinquent, deviant, and disordered means other ways to find health in less destructive ways.

Adolescents confuse us with their behaviors. They stubbornly stick to patterns that are dangerous to themselves and others. Understanding the good things that come from problems separates the young person from the problem. After all, the youth is not the problem, the problem behavior is the problem. Most adolescents willingly give up socially unacceptable patterns of behavior when more socially acceptable patterns that are just as satisfying are made available.

Much of what I've learned about how to help kids find health has been learned from kids themselves. It just takes patience and time if one is to learn about young people's lives from youth themselves.

The Questions We Need to Ask

The RYSI opens doors. It identifies areas of concern. It points us in the direction of a deeper understanding of our adolescents. So what happens then? What do we ask our kids in order to understand them better? The actual questions we ask are frequently less important than the attitudes we hold about our teens and the way we convey those attitudes as we ask them questions.

If we mean well and are genuinely curious about understanding our teenagers' lives on their terms, most teens will give us the time and attention we need as adults to understand how they survive and thrive. Our young people are willing to explain their lives when we adults are willing to listen with open minds.

I have many different types of questions I use to get conversations going. Here are some examples. I've included both general questions that might start a conversation and some more specific questions to follow up with when the teen begins talking. Of course, you can also return to the topics covered by the RYSI and simply ask about things you want to find out more about.

You can use these questions in any number of different combinations. They are simply teasers to get the conversation flowing. Feel free to change the wording to make them sound more the way you yourself speak.

- "If I were a kid today, what would I need to know to grow up well, to survive?"
- "How do you describe people like you and your friends who grow up well despite the many problems they face? What word(s) do you and your friends use? Is that the way I should think of kids today?"
- "What does it mean to you, to your family, to your teachers and others in your community, when bad things happen? What do you consider to be bad things?"
- "What kinds of things do you find most challenging growing up in your family, attending your school, and living in your community?"
- "What do you do when you face big problems in your life? What about little problems—what do you do then?"
- "What's it mean to be healthy?"
- "What do you do, and others you know do, to keep yourselves feeling good, mentally, physically, emotionally, spiritually?"
- "Can you share with me a story about another teen, maybe a friend or someone else you know at school, who has done really well even though he or she had lots of problems to overcome?"
- "What about you personally? Can you share a story with me about how you've managed to overcome the challenges you face at school, in your family, or in your community?"

Admittedly, if communication between you and a student in your classroom or under your counsel is blocked to the point where even these kinds of questions don't get a conversation going, it may be best to reach out for help. If you are a professional helper or caregiver, such as a counselor or foster parent, then chances are you have colleagues and other supports who can offer suggestions or even work with the youth on your behalf. If you're a teacher or parent of a nontalkative adolescent, then you may want to ask a professional counselor for assistance. After all, if you don't have a way to communicate with the teen, then it is unlikely you are going to know what that youth needs from you to sustain his or her well-being.

Conclusion

The Need for Change

Embracing a new perspective on youth is not easy. Much of our training as formal caregivers and teachers and much of our own upbringing and enculturation into our roles as parents have taught us to look at young people in one way and one way only. To see strengths beneath chaos so that we can more effectively help young people grow will demand a shift in our worldview.

That's not easy.

I'm reminded of Thoreau (1854/1962) who, when leaving Walden Pond, mused on the path his own footprints had worn walking from his cabin down to the pond and back again. He tells us, "The surface of the earth is soft and impressible by the feet of men [*sic*]; and so with the paths which the mind travels. How worn and dusty, then, must be the highways of the world, how deep the ruts of tradition and conformity" (p. 343).

We have been stuck with a way of thinking about youth that no longer serves us or them very well. We can do better. In fact, many of the strengths-based interventions now being used around the world demonstrate that we can help youth in ways that they will embrace. But we must be willing to shake off the shackles of our own conformity. No matter how radical we think ourselves as educators and mentors, trust youth in our care to challenge our complacency. Trust the panda to remind us of the need for constancy when demonstrating uniqueness. Trust the chameleon to demonstrate the need for flexibility. And trust leopards to offer us lessons in assertiveness. Now, those aren't bad prescriptions for resilience, are they?

References

Anderssen, E. (2004, October 9). Come on, get happy. *The Globe and Mail*, F1, F3.

Anthony, E. J. (1987). Risk, vulnerability, and resilience: An overview. In E. J. Anthony & B .J. Cohler (Eds.), *The invulnerable child* (pp. 3–48). New York: Guilford.

Bach, R. (1970). *Jonathan Livingston Seagull*. New York: Avon.

Carlson, R. (1997). *Don't sweat the small stuff...and it's all small stuff: Simple ways to keep the little things from taking over your life*. New York: Hyperion.

Chambon, A., & Irving, A., (Eds.). (1994). *Essays on postmodernism and social work*. Toronto: Canadian Scholars' Press.

Cross, W. E. (2003). Tracing the historical origins of youth delinquency and violence: Myths and realities about black culture. *Journal of Social Issues, 59*(1), 67–82.

Fallis, R. K., & Opotow, S. (2003). Are students failing school or are schools failing students? Class cutting in high school. *Journal of Social Issues, 59*(1), 103–119.

Foucault, M. (1980). *Power/knowledge*. C. Gordon, L. Marshall, J. Mepham, & K. Soper (Trans.). New York: Pantheon. (Original work published 1972)

Foucault, M. (1994). Truth and power. In J. D. Faubion (Ed.), *Michel Foucault: Power* (pp. 111–133). New York: The New Press. (Original work published 1976)

Frank, A. (1952). *Anne Frank: The diary of a young girl*. New York: Scholastic Book Services.

Fraser, M. (Ed.). (1997). *Risk and resilience in childhood: An ecological perspective*. Washington, DC: NASW Press.

Gergen, K. J. (2001). Psychological science in a postmodern context. *American Psychologist, 56*(10), 803–813.

Gergen, K. J., Hoffman, L., & Anderson, H. (1996). Is diagnosis a disaster? A constructionist trialogue. In F.W. Kaslow (Ed.), *Handbook of relational diagnosis and dysfunctional family patterns* (pp. 102–118). New York: John Wiley.

Gibran, K. (1982). *The prophet*. London: Heineman. (Original work published in 1923)

Gilligan, C. (1982). *In a different voice: Psychological theory and women's development*. Cambridge, MA: Harvard University Press.

Greene, R. (2002). *The concise 48 laws of power.* London: Profile Books.

Hansen, M. V., & Canfield, J. (1993). *Chicken soup for the soul.* Deerfield Beach, FL: HCI.

Jensen, D. (2002). *The culture of make believe.* New York: Context Books.

Kids Count (2004, October). Retrieved September 1, 2005, at http://www .aecf.org/kidscount/teen/overview/overview.htm

Ladner, J. A. (1971). *Tomorrow's tomorrow: The black woman.* Garden City, NY: Anchor.

"Loser" kills one at Alberta School. (1999, April 29). *The Daily News,* Halifax, Canada, p. 1.

Madigan, S. (1998). *Narrative therapy with Stephen Madigan: Family therapy with the experts* [Video series]. New York: Allyn & Bacon.

McNamee, S., & Gergen, K. J. (Eds.). (1992). *Therapy as social construction.* Thousand Oaks, CA: Sage.

Mitchell, J. (1970). The circle game. *Ladies of the canyon.* New York: Siquomb.

Moffitt, T. E. (1997). Adolescents—limited and life-course-persistent offending: A complementary pair of developmental theories. In T. P. Thornberry (Ed.), *Developmental theories of crime and delinquency* (pp. 11–54). New Brunswick, NJ: Transaction.

Morgan, A. (2000). *What is narrative therapy?* Adelaide, Australia: Dulwich Centre Publications.

Neill J. T., & Heubeck, B. (1998). Adolescent coping styles and outdoor education: Searching for the mechanisms of change. In C. M. Itin (Ed.), *Exploring the boundaries of adventure therapy: International perspectives* (pp. 227–243). Boulder, CO: Association for Experiential Education.

Nylund, D., & Ceske, K. (1997). Voices of political resistance: Young women's co-research on anti-depression. In C. Smith & D. Nylund (Eds.), *Narrative therapies with children and adolescents* (pp. 356–381). New York: Guilford.

Nylund, D., & Corsiglia, V. (1996). From deficits to special abilities: Working narratively with children labeled "ADHD." In M. F. Hoyt (Ed.), *Constructive therapies: Vol. 2* (pp. 163–183). New York: Guilford.

Olweus, D. (1993). *Bullying at school.* Oxford, UK: Blackwell.

Oxford English Dictionary (2nd ed.). (1989). London: Oxford University Press. Retrieved August 26, 2005, from www.askoxford.com

Pipher, M. (1994). *Reviving Ophelia: Saving the selves of adolescent girls.* New York: Ballantine.

Pollack, W. (1998). *Real boys: Rescuing our sons from the myths of boyhood.* New York: Henry Holt.

Rahey, L., & Craig, W. M. (2002). Evaluation of an ecological program to reduce bullying in schools. *Canadian Journal of Counselling, 36*(4), 281–296.

Salmivalli, C. (2001). Peer-led intervention campaign against school bullying: Who considered it useful, who benefited? *Educational Research, 43*(3), 263–278.

Sutton, J. (2001). Bullies: Thugs or thinkers? *The Psychologist, 14*(10). Retrieved September 1, 2005, at http://www.bps.org.uk/

Sutton, J., Smith, P. K., & Swettenham, J. (1999). Socially undesirable need not be incompetent: A response to Crick and Dodge. *Social Development, 8*(1), 132–134.

Taylor, J. M., Gilligan, C., & Sullivan, A. M. (1995). *Between voice and silence: Women and girls, race and relationship.* Cambridge, MA: Harvard University Press.

Thoreau, H. D. (1962). *Walden and other writings by Henry David Thoreau.* New York: Bantam. (Original work published in 1854)

Ungar, M. (2002). *Playing at being bad: The hidden resilience of troubled teens.* Lawrencetown Beach, Nova Scotia, Canada: Pottersfield.

Ungar, M., Lee, A. W., Callaghan, T., & Boothroyd, R. (in press). An international collaboration to study resilience in adolescents across cultures. *Journal of Social Work Research and Evaluation.*

Ungar, M., & Teram, E. (2000). Drifting towards mental health: High-risk adolescents and the process of empowerment. *Youth and Society, 32*(2), 228–252.

Venable, S. F. (1997). Adolescent rites of passage: An experiential model. *Journal of Experiential Education, 20*(1), 7–13.

White, M. (1988, Summer). The externalizing of the problem and the re-authoring of lives and relationships. *Dulwich Centre Newsletter,* 5–28.

White, M. (2000). *Reflections on narrative practice: Essays and interviews.* Adelaide, Australia: Dulwich Centre Publications.

White, M., & Epston, D. (1990). *Narrative means to therapeutic ends.* New York: Norton.

Whyte, W. F. (1943). *Street corner society.* Chicago: University of Chicago Press.

Winslade, J., & Monk, G. (1999). *Narrative counseling in schools: Powerful and brief.* Thousand Oaks, CA: Corwin.

Index

Acceptance, 4
Adaptation, providing opportunities for, 92
Andersen, E., 7
Anderson, H., 62
Anthony, E. J., 3
Antibullying campaigns, short-term, 90
Antismoking campaigns, 55
At-risk behaviors, substitutions for, 75-76. *See also* Drug use, substitutions for
Attachment disorder, 12, 62
Attention Deficit Hyperactivity Disorder (ADHD), 12

Bach, R., 35, 36, 40
Boothroyd, R., 99
Borderline personality disorder, 12
Bullies, viii, 39, 62-63, 82, 89-92
  as victims, 63
  building images of themselves, 92
  changing, 92
  coping and, 92
  power, 91, 92, 95
  See also Bullies, helping cope in non-bullying ways; Bullying
Bullies, helping cope in non-bullying ways, 82, 89-90, 93-94
  attack-back approach, 89, 90
  walk-away approach, 89, 90
Bullies, victims of, 81, 95
  substitutions for, 94-95
Bullying, viii, 7, 12, 81
  as coping, 82-88
  as point of pride, 85

as self-protection, 85
as social problem, 90
by girls, 55
occurring in context, 92
Bullying research, 92

Callaghan, T., 99
Canfield, J., 51
Carlson, R., 63
Car theft, 12. *See also* Delinquent behaviors; Delinquent youth
Ceske, K., 11
Chambon, A., 11
Chameleons, viii, 4, 13, 14, 24-28, 33, 37, 38, 62, 72, 78, 81, 92, 93, 99, 107, 118, 121
  as bully sidekicks, 91
  bullying victim as, 94
  changing identities, 25
  moral crisis and, 28
  positive characteristics, 27
  recognizing, 26-27
  Resilient Youth Strengths Inventory and, 113
Change:
  accepting invitations to, 10
  adult view, 5
  embracing, 5
  youth view, 5
Child and Youth Resilience Measure, 99. *See also* Resilient Youth Strengths Inventory
Choices, socially acceptable versus problem identity, 13-14
Collective conversations, 46
Columbine High School shootings, vii, 48
Constructed realities, 46-47

Consumerism, 78
  overt as bullying, 93
Coping, hidden. *See* Disadvantaged
    youth, hidden coping of
Corsiglia, V., 11
Craig, W. M., 90
Cross, W. E., 117
"Culture of make believe," 79
Cutting class:
  as coping mechanism, 52
Cyber communication, 55

Dangerous behaviors, viii, 37, 69, 82
  narrative interventions and, 11
  offering alternatives to, 7
  See also Dangerous youth
Dangerous youth, 11-12, 48, 50
Delinquent behaviors,
    viii, 37, 69, 82
  narrative interventions and, 11
  offering alternatives to, 7
  See also Delinquent youth
Delinquent youth, 12, 48, 50
Deviant behaviors, viii, 37, 69, 82
  narrative interventions and, 11
  offering alternatives to, 7
  See also Deviant youth
Deviant youth, 12, 48, 50
Disadvantaged youth, hidden coping
    of, 38-39. *See also* Identities
Discourses, 46
Disordered behaviors,
    viii, 37, 69, 82
  narrative interventions and, 11
  offering alternatives to, 7
  See also Disordered youth
Disordered youth, 12, 48, 50
Drug dealing, 12. *See also* Delinquent
    behaviors; Delinquent youth
Drug use, 7. *See also* Drug use,
    substitutions for
Drug use, substitutions for, 72-75
  meeting psychological needs, 73
  offering better way to rebel, 75
  using resilience strategies, 73-74
  youth employment, 74

Epston, D., 11

Fallis, R. K., 52
Foucault, M., 6, 46, 97
Fralick, Emmet, 48
Frank, A., 69

Fraser, M., 3

Gergen, K. J., 11, 62
Gibran, K., 5
Gilligan, C., 39, 70
Greene, R., 51

Hansen, M. V., 51
Harris, Eric, 48
Heubeck, B., 38
Hoffman, L., 62

Identities, 17-18, 32-34, 66, 94
  powerful, vii, viii, ix, 4, 7, 8, 9,
      15, 18, 30, 36, 39, 40, 51, 52, 54,
      55, 56, 61, 66, 71, 72, 76, 78, 79,
      94, 95, 97, 113
  providing opportunities to
      experiment with, 5
  See also Chameleons;
      Leopards; Pandas
Identity:
  finding one's, 66
  power of, 14
  See also Identities
Internet, surfing, 12
Invulnerables, 3
Irving, A., 11

Jensen, D., 79

Kids Count, 56
Klebold, Dylan, 48

Labeling youth:
  as excuse to rebel, 62
Labels:
  choosing, 6-7
  fighting "loser," 47
Ladner, J. A., 70
Lee, A. W., 99
Leopards, viii, 4, 13, 14, 28-32, 33, 37,
    38, 62, 72, 78, 81, 92, 93, 99, 107,
    118, 121
  as bullies, 91-92
  as defenders, 91
  as reformed bullies, 91
  distinguishing from pandas, 29-31
  positive characteristics, 30
  recognizing, 29
  Resilient Youth Strengths Inventory,
      113-117
Lesbian/gay/bisexual youth, 12

Madigan, S., 117
McNamee, S., 11
Mental health problems, 12. *See also*
  specific mental health problems;
  Deviant behaviors; Deviant youth;
  Disordered behavior; Disordered
  youth
Mitchell, J., 19
Moffitt, T. E., 55
Monk, G., 11, 111
Morgan, A., 11

Narcissistic personality
  disorder, 12, 62
Narrative interventions,
  11-13
Narrative therapists, 11
Neglect, 39, 40
Neill, J. T., 38
Nylund, D., 11

Olweus, D., 82, 92
Oppositional defiant disorder, 62
Opotow, S., 52
Oxford English Dictionary, 17

Pandas, viii, 4, 13, 14, 15, 18-25, 32, 33,
  37, 38, 62, 72, 78, 81, 92, 93, 99, 107,
  118, 121
  as bullies, 82, 88, 90, 93
  positive characteristics, 23-24
  powerful self-identity, 18, 24
  recognizing, 19
  Resilient Youth Strengths
    Inventory, 112
Pipher, M., 39
Playing at being bad, 72
Pollock, W., 39
Postmodern counseling, 11
Postmodernism, 46
Power, 4, 11, 14, 24, 25, 48, 57,
  66, 77, 79
  bully's, 91, 92, 95
  capillary, 6
  self-definition and, 6-7
Prostitution, 12. *See also* Delinquent
  behaviors; Delinquent youth

Rahey, L., 90
Resilience, 3-4, 7, 13, 16, 49
  conventional paths to, 38
  problem behaviors and, 6
  seeking, 115
  strategies to nurture, 36-37, 38, 50

unconventional paths to, 38
See also specific resilience strategies;
  Disadvantaged youth, hidden
  coping of; Resilience, assessing;
  Resilience, many expressions of
Resilience, assessing, 97-98, 107
  difficult teen, 108-109
  fairness, 107-109
  See also Resilient Youth Strengths
    Inventory
Resilience, many expressions of, 76-79
  political participation, 78
Resilience strategy 5—finding the
  difference that counts most,
  37, 61-67, 87
  advocating for individualized
    education and treatment
    plans, 61
  avoiding labeling youth, 61, 62
  nurturing large and varied
    "audiences" who appreciate
    youth's socially acceptable
    powerful identity, 61
  offering youth unique opportunities
    to show themselves as powerful
    and in control of their lives, 61
Resilience strategy 4—speaking in
  ways youth will hear and respect,
  37, 57-61, 86
  admitting own fears and aversion to
    risk, 57, 60, 61
  avoiding causing resistance when
    speaking to youth, 57, 59-61
  modeling how to respect one's truth
    respectful of others, 57
  offering unconditional
    compassion, 57, 61
Resilience strategy 1—hearing youths'
  truth and helping them listen for
  others', 36, 40-48, 85
  expressing curiosity, 40, 41
  listening well, 40, 41
  maintaining positive attitude
    toward youth, 40
  trying to understand world from
    youth's point of view, 40
Resilience strategy 6—substituting
  rather than suppressing,
  37, 66-67, 70-79
  offering youth new and more widely
    accepted stories to tell about
    themselves, 70-72
  playing audience to youths' new
    stories, 70

seeing youth problem behaviors as coping strategies, 70
See also At-risk behaviors, substitutions for; Drug use, substitutions for
Resilience strategy 3—creating opportunities that fit with what youth say they need, 36, 54-57, 85
helping youth realize barriers that face them as boys and girls and offer alternatives, 54, 55-56, 57
making possible socially acceptable outlets for identities, 54-55
recognizing barriers youth face in choosing healthy alternatives, 54, 57
Resilience strategy 2—helping youth look critically at their behavior, 36, 50-54, 86
asking youth how their behavior brings them powerful self-definitions, 50, 53-54
looking realistically at opportunities youth have to change and remain powerful, 50, 54
making new opportunities available as substitutes for problem behaviors, 50
showing tolerance for risk-taking behavior but offer safety structures, 50, 53
Resilient youth:
who beat the odds, 3
who more than beat the odds, 3
See also Invulnerables
Resilient Youth Strengths Inventory, viii-ix, 98-107
chameleons and, 113
filling in, 116-117
leopards and, 113-117
pandas and, 112
questions about community, 103-104
questions about culture, 105-106
questions about individual characteristics, 100-102
questions about relationships, 102-103
scoring, 106-107
translating results of, 111-118
using results to offer youth help, 118-120

Risk-taking behavior, 11-12. *See also* Dangerous behaviors; Dangerous youth

Salmivalli, C., 90
Self-definitions, powerful, 50, 53, 62, 93
Sexual promiscuity, 7
Shoplifting, 12. *See also* Delinquent behaviors; Delinquent youth
Smith, P. K., 92
Smoking, girls and, 56
Social misfits, 12. *See also* Deviant behaviors; Deviant youth
Status, vii, 7, 13, 14, 21, 23, 27, 53, 71, 74, 93, 95
Street youth, 12, 17-18
Strength-based interventions, 121
Substitution as intervention, 7-11, 25
chosen versus required alternative behavior, 13-14
competition from negative behavior, 14-15
purposes, 8
Suicide, 23, 24, 26
coping with bullying through, 48
Sullivan, A. M., 70
Survival strategies, 4-5. *See also* Chameleons; Leopards; Pandas
Sutton, J., 81, 92
Swettenham, J., 92
System, changing the:
while changing youth, 52-53

Taylor, J. M., 70
Teenage mothers, 70-71
Teram, E., 4
Thoreau, H. D., 121

Ungar, M., 4, 72, 99
Us-Them thinking, 5

Venable, S. F., 38
Violence, vii, viii, 17, 25, 40, 77, 81, 82, 89, 97, 103, 112
by girls, 56

White, M., 1, 11
Whyte, W. F., 54, 55
Winslade, J., 11, 111

YMCA drop-in center, 17-18

CORWIN PRESS

The Corwin Press logo—a raven striding across an open book—represents the union of courage and learning. Corwin Press is committed to improving education for all learners by publishing books and other professional development resources for those serving the field of PreK–12 education. By providing practical, hands-on materials, Corwin Press continues to carry out the promise of its motto: **"Helping Educators Do Their Work Better."**